JUNG
JOURNAL
CULTURE & PSYCHE

FALL

2007

VOLUME 1

NUMBER 4

SPECIAL ANNOUNCEMENT

THE UNIVERSITY OF CALIFORNIA PRESS
will publish JUNG JOURNAL,
beginning with the first issue in 2008.

We thank our wonderful community of subscribers, authors, artists, volunteers, and donors for making this possible. We plan to continue our hard work to make this a success for the Journal and for Jungian studies.

It is our hope that this new partnership will allow the Journal's articles to reach a wider audience, both abroad and in university and public libraries.

All subscriptions will be honored. When subscription management is transferred to UC Press, you will find a link on our home page, www.sfjungjournal.org.

Dyane Sherwood, EDITOR

Table of Contents

JUNG
JOURNAL
CULTURE & PSYCHE

FALL
2007
VOLUME 1
NUMBER 4

JUNG JOURNAL: CULTURE & PSYCHE, FALL 2007, VOL. 1, NO. 4, 4–6

Impressions of the XVII International IAAP Congress in Cape Town, South Africa

BY THOMAS B. KIRSCH

The International Association for Analytical Psychology, or the IAAP, is the international umbrella organization for all Jungian analysts in the world. Every three years, it organizes a week-long Congress where papers are presented in many different languages and on many different subjects around a given theme. It is also a time to renew international friendships and catch up with our colleagues from around the world. This year's conference theme was entitled "Journeys, Encounters: Clinical—Communal—Cultural," and the conference took place in Cape Town, South Africa. This was only the second time that a Congress has taken place outside of Europe or the United States. There was concern about how many people would make the long and expensive journey to South Africa, but in the end, more than 500 people attended the conference. The program committee had received numerous proposals so that concurrent papers, panels, and films were scheduled every afternoon except when the delegates met, making it impossible for any one participant to hear all the presentations. In the morning, the plenary sessions were open to all participants.

There were two unique features, besides location, to this Congress. One was the fact that local speakers from the surrounding community were invited to speak early on. The second was members of the Jungian academic community, the IAJS, were prominent speakers. For a country that experienced many years of apartheid, South Africa is now governed by the black majority. On the first morning of the Congress, we learned about the work of the Truth and Reconciliation Commission (TRC). Incredibly moving stories were told of what happened when perpetrators met with the families of the victims. This set the

THOMAS B. KIRSCH, M.D., is a psychiatrist in private practice in Palo Alto, California. He has served as president of the C.G. Jung Institute of San Francisco and of the International Association of Analytical Psychology (IAAP). He has written numerous articles and reviews and speaks frequently on clinical and historical topics. His book, *The Jungians*, has recently been translated into German, and he is the co-editor of *Initiation: The Living Reality of an Archetype*, published in 2007 by Routledge. *Correspondence:* 945 Middlefield Rd, Palo Alto, CA 94301 tone for the entire Congress, which was obvious from the moment that Cape Town was chosen as the location. We were all witness to the dramatic changes taking place as the blacks have an obvious majority and the white minority has chosen to stay and work things out. So far the experiment seems to be succeeding. We cannot, however, leave out the third large cultural group in South Africa—the "colored" group, which includes Indians, Malaysians, and other people of color, neither black nor white.

One evening of the conference was spent on reviewing Jung's travels in Africa. In 1925, Jung with three other companions set off on a six-month journey to Kenya, traveling to places where no white man had been before and having several brushes with death. It was a most significant journey for Jung among his many travels. Blake Burleson, a professor from Waco, Texas, has just published a book, *Jung in Africa,* that is both a travelogue and a psychological commentary of Jung's trip. Jung met Ruth Bailey on this trip, and she was to become a lifelong friend who came to live with him as his caretaker after Emma's death. The presentation of *Jung in Africa* was followed the next morning by a panel chaired by John Beebe, including Sam Kimbles, Michael Vannoy Adams, and a prominent photographer from South Africa, discussing the complexities of the cultural situation in Africa.

It would be hard to single out one or two papers from the Congress. The topics ranged from archetypal amplification to developmental issues to new ideas about the use of sand tray to training issues to simply talking about where we are as a profession today.

As the organization grows, the politics of the IAAP takes more time. The workload for those who become officers and serve on the executive committee has increased markedly. New election procedures, which have been in effect since 1998, have allowed for a more rapid turnover and for more people to get involved. One problem that needs to be looked at, however, is the election of the president elect. As it stands now, the two vice presidents usually run against each other, and the loser no longer has a place on the executive committee. This means that someone who has put a lot of energy into the IAAP can fall away completely. It is not a very good system. The choice of this Congress's delegates for the president-elect position was the American, Joe Cambray, an extremely hard worker and appropriate choice. It means that Cambray, who was the chair of the program committee of this Congress, will now serve as president elect for three years and then president for the following three years. Unfortunately, the candidate not chosen, Astrid Berg, no longer has any official capacity in the IAAP. It is particularly poignant because Astrid, as chair of the organizing committee, devoted herself to this Congress, and it was an extremely well-run Congress. The two new vice-presidents are Tom Kelly from Montreal and Jorge Rasche from Germany; Paul Kugler from Buffalo, New York, has been appointed honorary secretary.

Another important development of the IAAP is the growth of developing groups. There are now developing groups all over the world, and new analysts are emerging. A particularly moving moment was when the many newly certified Jungian analysts from Russia were introduced. There are now eighteen analysts in both St. Petersburg and Moscow, and they have formed an official IAAP group member society, the Russian Society of Analytical Psychology (RSAP). My wife Jean and I were first in Moscow and Leningrad (now St. Petersburg) in 1991 when interest in Jung emerged at the end of the Soviet era. The evolution of Jungian psychology in Russia has been a remarkable development involving many people from the IAAP.

The final afternoon of the Congress was also tremendously moving. Dancers as young as 1 1/2 and older were brought in from the township, and they gave a wonderfully natural presentation of music and dance from their own culture. Its authenticity was the absolute opposite of the commercially put-on "African Dance."

My sense at the end of the conference was that the participants were extremely satisfied with both the conference itself and the general ambience of being in Cape Town and that we were all pleased to be in South Africa. It was winter, at times raining and occasionally a cold wind blew across the two oceans, the Indian and the Atlantic, which meet at the Cape. It felt very far from home, and it turned our lives upside down.

JUNG JOURNAL: CULTURE & PSYCHE, FALL 2007, VOL. 1, No. 4, 7-8

Editor's Note: Early this year the poet Jane Hirshfield generously gave a reading to benefit JUNG JOURNAL. *It was a splended evening of poetry, engaging conversation, and storytelling. We are very grateful to Jane, to the Institute's Extended Education Director, Baruch Gould, and those who volunteered and attended, for creating a wonderful event and supporting the journal. In another act of generosity, Jane Hirshfield has given her permission to reprint two of her poems. We preface them with Patricia Damery's* Introduction *from the February 2007 event.*

Introduction to
Jane Hirshfield Benefit
for
JUNG JOURNAL: CULTURE & PSYCHE
February 2, 2007,
Fort Mason, San Francisco, California

PATRICIA DAMERY

Many years ago I took a poetry writing workshop at a bookstore in Marin called *A Clean Well-Lighted Place for Books*. I remember the day particulary well, in part because of the stark contrast between the brilliantly sunny, spring Sunday afternoon and the dark emotional space I was in. That morning I wondered if I even felt like taking the workshop, but I had taken some effort to submit poems and felt excited when I was accepted. So I went.

The workshop had about fifteen participants, and we sat around a long table. The teacher of the workshop would lecture briefly and then lead us in a writing exercise. We wrote for approximately fifteen minutes and then read what we'd written. We completed five cycles like this. Remarkably, when I left the workshop that afternoon, I felt better—whole and consolidated. The teacher of that workshop was, of course, Jane Hirshfield.

In preparing for this introduction, I looked through some of my notes from that workshop. Jane spoke about *voice* in a poem. She said:

PATRICIA DAMERY is an Analyst Member of the C.G. Jung Institute of San Francisco, the current Chair of the Jung Journal Committee, and a member of the Board of Governors. She is also a novelist and poet and raises lavender, grapes, and pygmy goats on her ranch in the Napa Valley. She has a private practice in Napa and has taught at Sonoma State University. *Correspondence:* 2337 Second St., Napa, CA. 94559, USA.

Voice is one way poetry creates and demands a connected self. Voice is the body language of a poem and does not lie.

Writing is an activity of soulmaking, the creation of yourself. Writing augments the Self.

Voice is the mirror and the maker of who we are, a way to expand who we are.

Jane distinguished between art and therapy, underscoring that what we were doing was art and not therapy. The differences are important. But I can say, that afternoon I experienced the intersection of the act of writing poetry and the analytical holding that happens in therapy that is so healing.

Jane is a highly intelligent, accessible, and quiet teacher whose own education and experience span her studies at Princeton University and her practice of Soto Zen. Although she's never been a full-time academic, she has taught at U.C. Berkeley, University of San Francisco, and in Bennington College's low-residency M.F.A. program, among other places. She has also worked as an editor on others' books, including Thomas Moore's *Care of the Soul* and Jack Kornfield's *A Path With Heart,* and has edited and cotranslated three books collecting the work of women poets from the past, including the now-classic *Women in Praise of the Sacred: 43 Centuries of Spiritual Poetry by Women.*

Her own poetry unflinchingly addresses almost intolerable emotions and eternal themes, including the transience of life and the mysteries of beauty, and in doing so, brings to the reader the experience of Presence. I say to analytical psychologists and analysands, "What more could we hope for as a product of our own work?"

Jane is author of six books of poetry and a collection of essays titled *Nine Gates, Entering the Mind of Poetry,* which I consider to be a primer for consciousness. She was finalist for the National Book Critics Circle Award and winner of the Poetry Center Book Award and the California Book Award. She has been the recipient of fellowships from the Academy of American Poets, the National Endowment for the Arts, and the Guggenheim and Rockefeller foundations.

Her work resists being defined in any one way. Of this she says, "When I published my own early books and the Japanese translations, I was called 'an erotic poet.' Now people tend to call me 'a spiritual poet.' No. I'm just a poet, just a human being, trying to see the full 360 degrees of this world."

And with that, I would like to welcome Jane Hirshfield.

JUNG JOURNAL: CULTURE & PSYCHE, FALL 2007, VOL. 1, NO. 4, 9-10

Two Poems by Jane Hirshfield

Flowering Vetch

Each of the tragedies can be read
as the tale of a single ripening self,
every character part of one soul.
The comedies can be included in this as well.
Often the flaw is a flaw of self-knowledge;
sometimes greed. For this reason
the comic glint of a school of herring leads to no plot line,
we cannot imagine a tragedy of donkeys or bees.
Before the ordinary realities, ordinary failures:
hunger, coldness, anger, longing, heat.
Yet one day, a thought as small as a vetch flower opens.
After, no longer minding the minor and almost wordless role,
playing the messenger given the letter
everyone knows will arrive too late or ruined by water.
To have stopped by the fig and eaten was not an error, then,
but the reason for going.

— Jane Hirshfield, *After,* New York: HarperCollins, 2006.

(Reprinted by permission of Jane Hirshfield)

Poet Jane Hirshfield's work has been described as "passionate and radiant" (*The New York Times Book Review*) "ethically aware" (*The Academy of American Poets*) and holding "a stunning physicality and the seductively rich music that such physicality engenders" (Kathleen Norris). Her many honors include fellowships from the Guggenheim and Rockefeller Foundations, the National Endowment for the Arts, and the Academy of American Poets. Her work has appeared in *The New Yorker* and *The Atlantic.* She is the author of six books of poetry, most recently *After* (HarperCollins, 2006), as well as a collection of essays, *Nine Gates: Entering the Mind of Poetry.*

Each Moment a White Bull Steps Shining into the World

If the gods bring to you
a strange and frightening creature,
accept the gift
as if it were one you had chosen.

Say the accustomed prayers,
oil the hooves well,
caress the small ears with praise.

Have the new halter of woven silver
embedded with jewels.
Spare no expense, pay what is asked,
when a gift arrives from the sea.

Treat it as you yourself
would be treated,
brought speechless and naked
into the court of a king.

And when the request finally comes,
do not hesitate even an instant--

Stroke the white throat,
the heavy, trembling dewlaps
you'd come to believe were yours,
and plunge in the knife.

Not once
did you enter the pasture
without pause,
without yourself trembling.
That you came to love it, that was the gift.

Let the envious gods take back what they can.

— Jane Hirshfield, *The Lives of the Heart,* New York: HarperCollins, 1997.
(Reprinted by permission of Jane Hirshfield)

JUNG JOURNAL: CULTURE & PSYCHE, FALL 2007, VOL. 1, NO. 4, 11-16

Flagging Patriotism:
The Myth of Old Glory

DEBRA MERSKIN

We can wear it, tear it, burn it, and inter it, but, after September 11, 2001, God forbid, we should question it—the American flag.[1] Flags epitomize the spirit of people and places and symbolically tell the world who "we" are and what "we" believe. Flags fly over and above; they are to be looked up to, toward, and at. Meaning is fluid, personal, and mythical. Individual interpretations of what a flag means is part of the pleasure afforded by freedom. However, a symbol, Joseph Campbell cautions in Pathways to Bliss, can be used manipulatively "when you have a dogma telling you what kind of effect the symbol is supposed to have upon you" (2004, 43). The American flag, which embodies mythic vision, has recently been used to define who belongs and who does not belong—who is one of "Us" and who is one of "Them."

In the five years following the September 11, 2001, attacks on the Pentagon and World Trade Center, the American flag-as-symbol became the American flag-as-sign. The concretization was quick. For days, New York City firefighters and police officers and other service personnel rummaged through the rubble of the two World Trade Center towers searching for the remains of missing bankers, brokers, lawyers, artists, and others of many nationalities. On September 11 itself, three firefighters who were searching for the missing in the rubble of the World Trade Center raised an American flag in front of the still smoking steel of the twin towers (see Figure 1). *New Jersey Record* photographer Thomas E. Franklin, who captured the moment in a picture that became a nation-defining image, recalled:

> I made the picture standing underneath what may have been one of the ele-
> vated walkways, possibly the one that had connected the World Trade plaza and
> the World Financial Center. As soon as I shot it, I realized the similarity to the
> famous image of the Marines raising the flag at Iwo Jima (See Figure 2). This was
> an important shot. It told more than just death and destruction. It said some-
> thing to me about the strength of the American people and of these firemen hav-
> ing to battle the unimaginable. ("The Photo Seen 'Round the World'")

Debra Merskin, Ph.D., is a graduate student in the Depth Psychology Program at Pacifica Graduate Institute. She is also an associate professor and sequence head for the Communication Studies Program in the School of Journalism & Communication at the University of Oregon. *Correspondence:* 214-C Allen Hall, Eugene OR 97403, USA. dmerskin@uoregon.edu

The Arlington National Cemetery web site also contains an interpretation of the photograph:

> Standing defiantly against the gray and white landscape of devastation, these dust-covered men and the vivid red, white, and blue of Old Glory instantly became a symbol of American patriotism. Neither the photographer nor the firefighters knew initially that their combined instincts would grow into a national symbol of patriotism. (Arlington National Cemetery, ¶2)

Figure 1. *Firemen Raise the American Flag at the Ruins of the World Trade Center, New York, September 11, 2001. (Thomas E. Franklin, 2001, by permission, New Jersey Record)*

The press also noted the parallels between the 2001 image and the famous 1945 photograph taken by Joe Rosenthal at Iwo Jima, and so a powerful symbolic image from the past, recalling an unprovoked attack from a far-off enemy, as well as heroism and victory at great sacrifice, began to define the meaning of the attack on the World Trade Center in patriotic terms that required neither self examination nor any attempt to grasp the realities of the contemporary world situation. Almost immediately, daily newspapers provided printed inserts of Old Glory suitable for framing. For months following the tragedy, flags (made in China) flew off store shelves and onto car bumpers, t-shirts, buttons, bras, badges, and lawn signs as emblems of patriotism. The flag was similarly used as a creative strategy in countless advertisements. Public proclamations of patriotism, such as "America, my country right or wrong," were uttered alongside President George W. Bush's September 2001 address to a Joint Session of Congress, in which he stated, "Every nation, in every region, now has a decision to make. Either you are with us, or you are with the terrorists." A new law, which encroached on the very civil liberties that the flag represented to many, was called "The Patriot Act." There was only one way to define patriotism, one "true" leader, and one true "way," and Franklin's iconic photograph pulled on our emotions to identify with these heroes and to agree with the stance that called upon this image as a mandate. In "True Victory," Barbara Brown Taylor writes:

> Now that the war against terrorism is well underway, things have eased up a little [...] a month ago, you could not walk into a room full of people without someone trying to pin a flag on your lapel. If you refused, or even hesitated, you were treated to such a narrowing of the eyes that you got a sense of what it must have been like to be a suspect during the McCarthy era, or an early Christian in Rome. The pressure to salute the state was so great that it felt dangerous not to. (2001, 23)

This effort on the part of individuals to maintain group cohesiveness is an example of what Thomas Singer and Samuel Kimbles refer to as a "cultural complex" (2004, 176). Whereas individuals seek a sense of kinship and belonging, groups exhibit the same desire for self-defining connectedness. According to this argument, just as individuals have a shadow side, so do groups, and although community spirit can be positive, it can become pathological "in archetypal defense[s] of the group spirit" (201).

Symbolizing Solidarity

Human beings are symbol makers and symbol seekers. In Thou Art That, Joseph Campbell cautions us about the power that symbols have to define how and what we think:

A real danger exists when social institutions press on people mythological structures that no longer match their

FIGURE 2. *"Raising the Flag on Iwo Jima." (Joe Rosenthal/ Associated Press, 1945, by permission).*

human experience. For example, when certain religious or political interpretations of human life are insisted upon, mythic dissociation can occur. Through mythic dissociation, persons reject or are cut off from effective explanatory notions about the order of their lives. (2001, 5)

When "mythology is misused ... as direct history, symbol becomes fact, metaphor dogma" (Campbell 2002a, 53). Furthermore, according to Jung, "dogma expresses an irrational whole by means of imagery" (CW 11 ¶81; Campbell 2002a, 56)

Campbell succinctly contrasted sign and symbol when he wrote that symbols are "the best possible allusion to something unknown" and "a reference to some concept or object definitely known" (2002a, 99). Symbols give structure and meaning to life, but they can be appropriated into effective tools of intolerance, coercion, and control, representing the societal-level shadow of Jung's collective unconscious. The Swastika, for example, is an ancient symbol with great religious significance in Hinduism, Jainism, and Buddhism. Under Hitler, however, who, according to Campbell, "was a genius at employing ritual to develop national consciousness" (95), its meaning became solidified as sign, signifying racial supremacy, power, and fascism as ideals. In Nazi Germany, individual self-image and conceptions of social solidarity were constructed in ways that formed rigid barriers of inclusiveness and exclusiveness (Campbell et al. 1974, 243).

Containing Consciousness

In the months and years since 9/11, symbols—verbal and visual—of faith, freedom, and compassion have filled contemporary popular culture and the popular imagination. Because it is such a common part of our visual environment, the flag has been the perfect container for fixing and conveying the intended message of conformity, consensus, and

> [...] can be viewed without the effort of conscious interpretation. It reductively references "America." The flag is a symbol of national unity; it is the "idea" of the ideal nation, of the principles of its foundation, not the nation itself. (Clark and Hoynes 2003, 443)

In *The Inner Reaches of Outer Space,* Campbell asserts, "mythology is not [...] ideology," yet he later discusses the potential of myth to be a "control system [...] framing its community" (2002b, xix; xxiii). Mythology can be used as a mechanism of social control, simplistically defining countries as "good" and "evil," using the flag as a tangible signifier of a moral imperative to war, and thus labeling as unpatriotic anyone who questions this moral certainty. This process is similar to the power of concretized religious myths and signs used to construct *a single* truth and *a single* god. The flag—ideally an abstract representation of a set of ideals, a mythology, national identity, symbol of loyalty, belief, unity, and a source for inspiration—has instead been reified, fulfilling what became known as the Spears [as in Britney] standard: "I think we should just trust the president in every decision he makes" (LaBossier 2006). The flag now insists we do that.

According to Campbell, "myths are productions of the human imagination," but what happens when that imagination fails? What happens when a people's history is told and retold within a framework dedicated to social control, and if myths operate in two ways, bearing "psychological, but at the same time metaphorical, connotations," what happens if the psychic balance is thrown off by "tribal literalism" (2002b, 29; 31)? According to Campbell, "In the popular nightmare of history, where local mythic images are interpreted, not as metaphors, but as facts, there have been ferocious wars waged between the parties of such contrary manners of metaphoric representation" (30).

Consequently, Terry Tempest Williams writes, "our language has been taken hostage," particularly "words like patriot, patriotism, democracy, and liberty, have been bound and gagged, forced to perform indecent acts through the abuse of slogans. *Freedom will prevail. We are liberating Iraq. God bless America"* (2004, 1. Italics from original). Campbell acknowledges that, just like religious belief systems, secular myths can be used to "reinforce a certain moral order and shape a people or individual to it" (2001, 5). When the mystical, psychological, pedagogical, and sociological functions of myth become mechanisms for social control, we relinquish our mythic capacity. Campbell asserts that, "the life of mythology springs from, and depends on, a metaphoric vigor of its symbols. The symbol, energized by metaphor, conveys some realization of the infinite" (6). Concretizing a symbol into a single vision thereby stilts the energy that would have gone into imagining possibilities—and the symbol dies. Thus, the unilateral vision of the Bush administration's vision of who and what is patriotic "devalues the symbol," while demonstrating the power of myth to channel the nation's energies toward the accomplishment of a one-dimensional set of political beliefs (20).

The potential for "inner space," a personal interpretation of liberty, is concretized when the symbol (flag) becomes the sign for a reflexive action rather than an interpretive process (Campbell 2002b, 20). The "denotation instead of the connotation" is taken "as the term of the message, [...] the transcendent message" (2001, 19). In *War is a Force that Gives us Meaning,* foreign war correspondent Chris Hedges writes:

> States at war silence their own authentic and humane culture. When this destruction is well advanced, they find the lack of critical and moral restraint useful … by destroying authentic culture—that which allows us to question and examine ourselves and our society—the state erodes the moral fabric. It is replaced with a warped version of reality. [...] National symbols—flags, patriotic songs, sentimental dedications—invade and take over cultural space. Art becomes infected with the platitudes of patriotism. (2002, 63)

In *Birth of Tragedy Nietzsche* notes,

> [W]ithout myth every culture loses the healthy natural power of its creativity: only a horizon defined by myth completes and unifies a whole cultural movement. And now the mythless man stands eternally hungry, surrounded by all past ages, and digs and grubs for roots. (1999, 109)

Americans are hungry for and in need of "mythic renewal" (Jacobi 1974, 117). Our task now is to cultivate "inner space" (Campbell 2002b, 20), to strengthen the "connective tissue" of group life (Singer and Kimbles 2004, 184), to return to the collective "marsupial pouch" (Campbell 2004, 19), and to disrupt the solidification of cultural meaning based upon in the interpretations of a powerful few.

ENDNOTE

1. A 1968 "federal law provided penalties of as much as a year's imprisonment or a $1,000 fine or both for publicly burning or otherwise desecrating any U.S. flag. In addition, many states have laws against flag desecration. However, in 1989, the Supreme Court ruled that no laws could prohibit political protesters from burning the flag. The decision had the effect of declaring unconstitutional the flag desecration laws of 48 states, as well as a similar federal statute, in cases of peaceful political expression." In June 1990, "the Supreme Court declared a new federal law making it a crime to burn or deface the American flag violated the free-speech guarantee of the First Amendment. The 5-4 Court decision led to renewed calls in Congress for a constitutional amendment to make it possible to prosecute flag burners (*World Almanac & Book of Facts,* 2006, 589–590).

BIBLIOGRAPHY

Arlington National Cemetery. "Old Glory Raised at New York's World Trade Center." http://www.arlingtoncemetery.net/fireman-01.htm (accessed April 18, 2006).

Brown Taylor, Barbara. 2001. "True Victory." *Christian Century,* 118.

Bush, George W. September 20, 2001. "Address to a Joint Session of Congress and the American People." http://www.whitehouse.gov/news/releases/2001/09/20010920-8.html (accessed May 18, 2006).

Campbell, Joseph, Duane Elgin, Willis Harman, Arthur Hastings, O. W. Markley, Floyd Matson, Brendan O'Regan, and Leslie Schneider. 1974. "Changing Images of Man." Report for The Charles F. Kettering Foundation, Menlo Park, CA: Center for the Study of Social Policy.

Campbell, Joseph. 2001. *Thou Art That: Transforming Religious Metaphor.* Novato, CA: New World Library.

——. 2002a. *Flight of the Wild Gander.* Novato, CA: New World Library.

——. 2002b. *The Inner Reaches of Outer Space: Metaphor as Myth and Religion.* Novato, CA: New World Library.

——. 2004. *Pathways to Bliss: Mythology and Personal Transformation.* Novato, CA: New World Library.

Clark, Claire and William Hoynes. 2003. "Images of Race and Nation after September 11." *Peace Review* 15.

"Code of Etiquette for Display and Use of the U.S. Flag." 2006. *World Almanac & Book of Facts,* 2006.

Hedges, Chris. 2002. *War Is a Force that Gives Us Meaning.* New York: Public Affairs.

Jacobi, Jolande. 1974. *Complex, Archetype, Symbol in the Psychology of C. G. Jung.* Trans. Ralph Manheim. New York: Princeton University Press.

Jung, C.G. 1984. "Psychology and Western Religion." CW 11, ¶81.

LaBossier, Michael. 2006. "Provocations: Patriot Games." *TPM Online: The Philosopher's Magazine* (May 10), http://www.philosophersnet.com/cafe/archive_article. php?id=30&name=provocations.

Nietzsche, Frederick. 1999. *The Birth of Tragedy and Other Readings.* New York: Cambridge University Press.

Singer, Thomas and Samuel L. Kimbles. 2004. "Emerging Theory of Cultural Complexes." *Analytical Psychology: Contemporary Perspectives in Jungian Analysis.* Ed. Joseph Chambray and Linda Carter. New York: Brunner-Routledge.

Tempest Williams, Terry. 2004. "Commencement." *The Open Space of Democracy (New Patriotism).* Great Barrington, MA: The Orion Society.

"The Photo Seen 'Round the World.'" 9/11: *Pop Culture and Remembrance.* <http://sept-terror.tripod.com/firephoto.html>.

ABSTRACT

DEBRA MERSKIN. "Flagging Patriotism: The Myth of Old Glory." JUNG JOURNAL: CULTURE & PSYCHE, 1:4, 11-16. When does a symbol become a sign? Did the meaning of the American flag change after 9/11? This essay explores the use of the American flag as a mythological image and hegemonic tool used to define who is one of "Us" and who is one of "Them." For example, President George W. Bush's statement, "Every nation, in every region, now has a decision to make. Either you are with us, or you are with the terrorists." The author posits that symbols, verbal and visual, of faith, freedom, and compassion filled contemporary popular culture and the popular imagination and became concretized into uniform signs. Symbols give structure and meaning to life, but they can be appropriated into effective tools of intolerance, coercion, and control, representing the societal-level shadow of Jung's collective unconscious. Because it is such a common part of our visual environment, the flag is the perfect container for fixing and conveying the intended message of conformity and consensus. It speaks to Americans' hunger and need for "mythic renewal."

KEY WORDS

Patriotism, flag, symbol, sign, myth, ideology, collective unconscious, cultural complex, 9/11

What is this strange sphere that Kircher places at the heart of the volcano?

Underground spring. Kircher believed there was a vast network of waterways and springs beneath the Earth's surface. Image is photographed from Kircher, *(MS [Mundus subterraneus]*, Bk. V, 291).

JUNG JOURNAL: CULTURE & PSYCHE, FALL 2007, VOL. 1, NO. 4, 18–31

The Earth Is an Alembic

an 'imaginal' reading of the images in

Athanasius Kircher's

d'ONDER-AARDSE
WEERELD
or *Mundus subterraneus*
[Atlas of the Underworld]

Athanasius Kircher (1662–1680), *Mundus subterraneus*
[Atlas of the Underworld], XII libros digestus,
Amsterdam, Janssonio-Waesbergiana, 1678.

DOROTHY NISSEN

For Kircher...cosmic bonding is the most basic physical expression of the idea that God is Love; even the rocks and the planets love one another.... [As is true for Giordano Bruno] ... the entire universe [is] infused with a great...world-soul that extend[s] to infinity, an emanation of the infinite power of divinity. (Rowland 2000, 74)

Athanasius Kircher's *Mundus subterraneus* of 1678 is a book that belonged to my father. My father, a sensible man, was interested in the book as a natural history and regarded its many alchemical images as a detriment to its credibility as a scientific document. I have lived with this book since I was a child, and in many ways it became a vessel for the redemption of my relationship with my father.

DOROTHY NISSEN, MFA, is a painter and book artist who also works as a graphic designer. The series of prints shown above right, *Caves, Awe, and My Mother and Father,* combines photographs of her ancestral family — many from the late 1800s — with images from a book of her father's, Athanasius Kircher's 1678 *Subterranean Atlas,* in a personal attempt at "cosmic bonding." *Correspondence:* dorothynissen@comcast.net or 1012 Creston Rd., Berkeley, CA 94708. See www.studiodotwiz.com

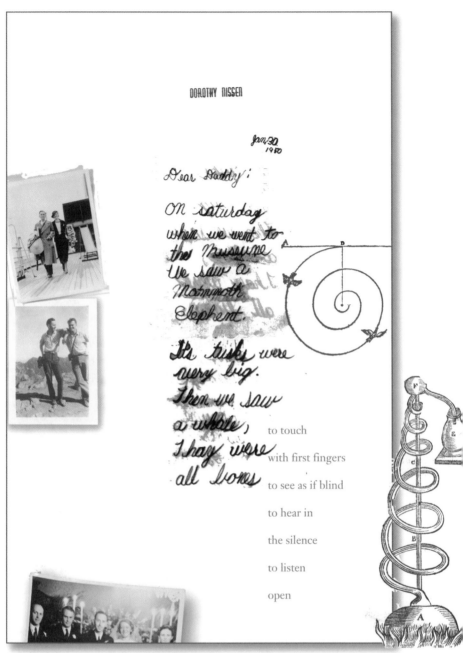

DOROTHY NISSEN

Jan 30.
1950

Dear Daddy;

On saturday
when we went to
the Museume
we saw a
Mammoth
Elephant.

Its tusks were
very big.
Then we saw
a whale,
They were
all Lions

to touch

with first fingers

to see as if blind

to hear in

the silence

to listen

open

To touch with first fingers; a seven-year-old's letter to her distant father. (Was this an attempt to bond with him through a shared feeling of awe toward nature?) The spiral path of the bird's flight is from the first book of the twelve which is entitled *Middelpunt's Beschryving [Describing the Midpoint].* To me this referred to the act of locating the center of the Earth, the *Axis Mundi.* My father's interest in maps and old books may have been driven by the death of his immigrant father when he was just two. He cannot have known him, and surely he spent many hours imagining and locating his own place of origin. For me the spiral vessel shown on the right is a *calcinatio* image having to do with linking these original emotions (of longing) with their archetypal source. (In fact this image is from Book IV, *Beschryvende de Wateren,* and seems to be an apparatus for extracting salt from sea water.) *(MS,* Bk. IV, 200).

A self-avowed mystic and scientist, Kircher took his chair in Mathematics at the Jesuit Order's Collegio Romano, which (with some synchronistic prevision) had been built on top of the ruins of an ancient temple of Isis. It was 1635, just two years after Galileo had been charged with "vehement suspicion of heresy" for espousing the Copernican view that the Earth circles the Sun, and it was just weeks after Galileo's sentence had finally been commuted to house arrest (Rowland 2000, 1).

Kircher's 1656 *Itinerarium exstaticum* is a fictional account of a Dantesque journey to the outer reaches of a Sun-centered cosmos. Under the pseudonym Theodidactus *(divinely taught)*, Kircher is guided by an angel named Cosmiel *(honeyed thing)*, whose words are said to be more acerbic than his name implies. Ever honing his skill at poetic subterfuge, Kircher managed to avoid more concrete allusion to his agreement with Copernicus. When expedience demanded, he called upon his Jesuit devotion and obedience to obfuscate contradictions in the view in which he was trained — that is, Tycho Brahe's Earth-centered universe, in which the Sun, orbited by the planets other than Earth, orbits the Earth and fixed stars. At other times he illustrated Newton's ideas on gravity and shared Kepler's view of a central fire in the Earth. Kircher frequently declares his Christian devotion, yet he presents many conflicting ideas, including a complex theory of correspondences (see page 30). A person of prodigious interests and learning, Kircher pretended more knowledge — in philology, for example — than he actually possessed. His translation of the Egyptian hieroglyphs on the Pamphili Obelisk that had been exhumed from the sanctuary of Isis beneath the Collegio — as well as his insistence on the existence of secret links between pagan and Christian beliefs — were declared by no less than Leibniz to have been simply made up. It must be said in Kircher's defense though, that his sources in the case of the obelisk were themselves simulacra, the key one having been copied from a prior manuscript by someone with no knowledge of the language

Kircher was not only a showman, but a formidable designer and packager of books. He published more than forty handsome tomes, all the while producing a staggering array of baroque spectacles that entailed magic lanterns, a working clock in the form of a mechanically-heliotropic sunflower, and other illusionistic devices (Findlen 2004, 6).

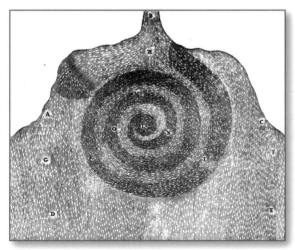

BELOW: Representation from exhumed bones of underearth giant compared to historically known giants..

Frontispiece of the 1678 Dutch edition. Curiously, the first row of horned animals on the goddess's skirt are antlered deer; the other two rows are the bulls one associates with more Mediterranean cultures.

The Frontispiece d'Onder-Aardse Weereld *anticipates the book's contents*

D'Onder-Aardse Weereld in Twaalf Boeken Natuurkundig Verhandeld [The Underground World. A Physics Treatise in Twelve Books] is the 1678 post-humous Dutch translation of *Mundus subterraneus,* first published in Latin in 1665. In the frontispiece of this second edition (shown on the left), a statue of the many-breasted Artemis, similar to the one at Ephesus except for the reindeer adorning the first row of her skirt, presides over a scene in which a woman, perhaps Kircher's muse or alter-ego, is attended by three figures: Hermes holds a wand-like caduceus over her head, and is himself assisted by a radiant figure who could be Apollo, but whose rays may be the *panspermian* energy Kircher believed emanated from the Sun itself. Kircher took the idea of *panspermia,* the universal seed, from Giordano Bruno, who had been burned at the stake by the Inquisition in 1600, not for his Copernican astronomy but for "obstinance." Kircher wisely concealed some of his favorite sources, however, especially if they were on the papal Index (Rowland 2004, 196). To the left of the female scribe, a winged puti holds up a portrait of Kircher as if to suggest that the scribe is mediating or channeling Kircher's energy. The presence of Hermes together with Apollo in a chamber ruled by Artemis, the goddess of the Moon, suggests that somehow the empirical method — proposed by Aristotle and promoted in Kircher's Jesuit education (as long as it complied with the idea of an Earth-centered universe) — will be conjoined in this work with another form of knowledge whose source, alchemical or not, is the hermetic arts. Through an archway in the background, a cave is revealed in which stone workers wielding pick axes are working to uncover the messages etched into the walls of the cave. Does this reflect the alchemical belief that the elements in stones come from meteorites that are actually fallen gods? The elements in alchemy carry the attributes of these gods; copper carries and expresses desire, and so on (Coudert 1980). Behind the statue of Artemis is an opening to a second room, a laboratory in which a robed man, perhaps a magus, conducts experiments at the hearth of a fireplace. He is surrounded by various alembics and vessels and books.

The handwriting in stones in Kircher's **Mundus subterraneus**

The first book of *Mundus subterraneus* is not a mathematical locating of the the Earth's center, as I had imagined, but rather an attempt at a mathematical proof of Tycho Brahe's theory that the Sun orbits the Earth; the second book describes the gravitational relationship of the Sun, Moon, and tides; the third book explores the nature of water and the oceans; the fourth, the power of undergound fire; the fifth, underground springs, fountains, and seas; the sixth, minerals that come from water; and the seventh, mining and metallurgy. The subject of the eighth book, *Handelende van de Steenige Stof des Aardryks,* is the behavior of the "stoney stuff" in the Earth, in other words, paleontology. It is in this book that Kircher seems most reckless (or divinely-driven) in practicing his own art of combining observation with confabulation. Deeply embedded in a baroque worldview in which notions of divinely-wrought spontaneous generation and other aspects of evolution were in a lively state of revision in the basement laboratories of ecclesiastical centers of learning, Kircher appears to believe that fossils not only record geological history, but also prevision mythical and human history as well. He appears to imagine evolution as a process that is fueled by human and divine imagination, mimesis and experiment. Late in the book, in a contrasting feeling tone, he reveals an expansively comic view of alchemical apparatus and process (see below right from Bk. XII).

the miners approached the mines with stealth, fearful that they would bring out a living, breathing thing before its rightful time

LEFT: Placing the mineshaft beneath the trails of a Tilden hillside where I often walk, I thought of the words of Walter Clive who is quoted in Allison Coudert's *The Philosopher's Stone:* "The miners approached the mines with stealth, fearful that they would bring out a living, breathing thing before its rightful time." (1980, 200) *(MS,* Bk. X, *"Van de Gelegentheid der Mynen" [The Location and Development of Mines])*

RIGHT: An *anima*-ted view of alchemical process. *(MS,* Bk.XII, 346)

Kircher's view of alchemy

Kircher's expressed view of alchemy is much more antagonistic than that of his contemporary Sir Isaac Newton (who practiced alchemy in his spare time between writing treatises on religion, and — what were of less importance to him personally — treatises on the laws of mechanical physics).

Kircher is known for mocking alchemy and reviling, while at the same time borrowing from, Paracelsus. Rowland does not speak of Kircher as an alchemist, but in a book published before the flurry of interest in Kircher in the 1990s, Jocelyn Godwin describes as an alchemist. Godwin classifies alchemists into four types:

> (1) those who believe transmutation impossible but conduct chemical experiments for other purposes; (2) the metallurgists; (3) sellers of imitation gold and silver; (4) those who for personal gain fraudulently pretend to achieve transformation. He himself was of the first category; clearly he was fascinated by chemistry. ... He wrestled inconclusively with the two standard divisions of substance: the classical quaternary of earth, water, air and fire, and the Paracelsian ternary of salt, sulphur and mercury, wanting to accept them both but unable to make the mental bifurcation necessary to accept two different levels or modes of being (Godwin 1979, 85).

Kircher witnessed the eruption of Mount Ætna in 1637. He wrote that it was the profound emotional impact of this experience that caused him to shift his focus from philology and mathematics to the empirical sciences. Surely the idea of a central subterranean fire — which he took from Kepler — was also a core inspiration for this book — along with his notion of a vast network of underground waterways nourishing the planet. Soon after he wrote Turris Babel *[Tower of Babel]. Could this choice of topics be a response to the conflicting voices that emerged in writing* Mundus subterraneus? *In either case, it seems that his conversion to empirical observation, which had been occasioned by viewing the eruption of this volcano, was not permanent!*

Why does Kircher seem so alchemically-minded then, when he attacked the alchemists?

A split is often seen between the Platonic worldview that is for some the jumping off point for the modern form of Western thought emerging in the Enlightenment period, and Presocratic thought with its various pre-alchemical ideas: initially of a single originary *material* element — Thales's water, Heraclitus's fir[e] well as flux), and Anaximenes's air; at rough[ly] same time, the more *idealist* notion of an orig[inary] substance — Anaximander's *apeiron* and Par[men]ides's *nöos;* and finally, the idea of four elem[ents] introduced by Empedocles. This *split* must [have] been experienced as a kind of continuu[m] the seventeenth century worldview. Ever[y]

...ceptual organization of Kircher's *Atlas of the Underworld* is steeped in alchemical ideas.

The more striking dichotomy in the ...nteenth century worldview, however, is revealed ...he tension between belief in church doc-...e and an increasing fascination with science. ...ording to Thomas van Leeuwen, "in the ...ner so typical of ecclesiastic scholarship...

Kircher existed in a kind of dream state, a succession of hallucinations, where hallucination and objectivity are forced to go hand-in-hand" (2004). *Hallucination?* ... Perhaps it was the idea of the universal seed, *panspermia*, that Rowland traces to Bruno and to Aristotle's *entelechia*, that enabled him to navigate between these contradictory realms with unflagging humor (2004, 196-8).

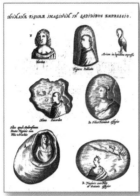

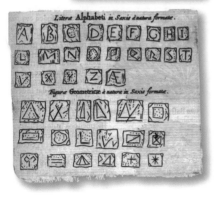

TOP LEFT: In the images shown on the left Kircher seems to associate mummification with the evolution of the chrysalis. Perhaps these images reflect his belief in *palingenesis,* the transmigration of souls, since the caption shown at the right seems to say "all things can be transformed (become other) in stones!"

Alle dingen konnen in steen veran- deren.

LEFT: ***Human faces imagined in the expression of stones.*** Kircher shows how fossils record and prevision human history. According to Stephen Jay Gould, Kircher did believe in certain instances of spontaneous generation (Gould 2004, 210).

BELOW LEFT: The last image below seemed to me to say that the alphabet and geometric forms are divine signs written in stone and given to us by the angels (*MS,* Bk. VIII, *Van de Steenen [On Stones],* 21). At the same time *Mundus subterraneus* has many illustrations of fossils that were formed naturally.

The Earth is an alembic

Kircher's *Atlas of the Underworld* seems to imagine the Earth itself as an alembic. This idea, along with his shift in focus to the natural sciences, *could* well have seized him when he witnessed the eruption of Mount Ætna in 1637. The fact that the Earth's creation and existence are miraculously improbable *even from the most scientific perspective,* and that its survival requires our attentive participation, is an idea that is crucial in our own time of ecological crisis.

When I first tried to parse the meaning of this book, it seemed to trace an alchemical process, that is, an attempt to reconcile certain opposites within the author. Although I cannot read the Dutch text and can only parse the Latin captions with a reckless and playful use of guess work, I feel a deep connection with the view expressed in at least the wholeness of this book that the geological Earth *is* a wondrous alembic as it undergoes changes in temperature and pressures within. In these pages I wanted to make a connection between the awe, as well as a kind of atavistic darkness, that I felt as a child in relation to my parents and a feeling that our lineage as humans reaches back to the earliest geological life in our planet eons before human existence.

Conclusion: My Father, Kircher and Me, ... and Who?

Last night, perhaps in response to the need I have been feeling to make a coherent ending and therefore narrative for this article, I dreamt that the nipple of my left breast was bleeding during a meeting I had with Kircher's colleague Gaspar Schott. Was I slighting some feminine aspect of myself by leaving no room for a feeling conclusion to this article, by not saying just *how* this book somehow redeemed my father for me? Schott, whom I am meeting with in the dream, was Kircher's assistant, apologist, in my mind, his lover, and probably the person on whom the angel Cosmiel, Kircher's guide in *Ecstatic Journey,* was based (Rowland 2000, 21-22). He was an excellent experimentalist upon whom Kircher relied for the working out of his ideas, and was no less a person of great acumen, since it is he who urged Kircher to write something that would reveal his Copernican view of astronomy. That something turned out to be the *Itinerarium exstaticum coeleste [Ecstatic Celestial Journey],* the fictional account discussed on page 21, which was based on a visionary dream Kircher actually had — as he tells the story — of a journey to the outer reaches of a universe *in motion.* It was only some years later in Schott's annotated re-publication of this book, newly entitled *Ecstatic Journey,* that mention was made of Kircher's intellectual indebtedness to Giordano Bruno. Moreover this fictional *Itinerarium exstaticum* was Kircher's only foray into the endangered area of Copernican astronomy.

With his extroverted focus on circumventing censure (though *Ecstatic Journey* was itself soon added to the Index), Kircher

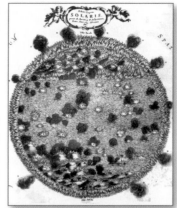

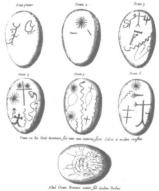

TOP: *Solaris.* A map of the solar fires Kircher was able to observe through his telescope.

CENTER: *The Moon.*

BOTTOM: *The creation in seven days.*

Perhaps this is an allusion to *panspermia,* the universal seed that emanates from the Sun and inseminates the earthly world.

Page for my Mother. I loved Kircher's image of the Virgin and Child found "expressed" in a geode-like stone. Kircher apparently agrees with the Gnostic view that at least one of the Marys went to live in a cave in Southern France. I am not sure it was the Mother of God, though it is She who "kept these things and pondered them in her heart," (as one might do in a cave). In retrospect I think that my idea in this print was to show that one's own/my own body comes from a chthonic source.

My Cousins in Tonder in Southern Denmark. When I met my cousins during the summer before I entered high school, one was a Lutheran minister and the others were farmers. Their lives were close to the Earth, and their animals were kept in a shed near the kitchen for warmth. It is for this reason that I included Kircher's imaginary fossil of a human hand that I tinted green. Of the central image Kircher seemed to me to say that the alphabet and geometric forms are divine signs that come to us from the angels and are written in stones.

BELOW FROM LEFT: *My Father's Father* with his passport from 1875 and Kircher's *Fornax Spagyrica* (actually an ecclesiastic still!). *My Mother's Mother* who read constantly (Austin and Dickens), according to my mother, and forgot to serve the recipes she cooked from the Sear's mail order catalog. *My Father's Mother Augusta* who left home and came west by herself on a train from Cincinnati when she was nineteen. Her photograph is layered with the receipt for the Steinway grand piano she managed to import from Hamburg in 1901 and Kircher's image of a bird with a serpent's tail which to me represents Mozart's Papageno — my father played the flute.

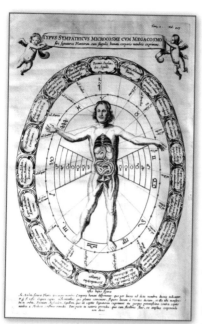

Theory of correspondences. For Kircher, the structure of the microcosm of the body reflects that of the macrocosm of the heavens. This chart shows the sympathetic relationship between various medicinal plants and herbs, parts of the body, the astrological signs, and the heavens.

instead generally defended Tycho Brahe's compromise cosmic structure. Of equal or more offense to the church than the idea of a Sun-centered universe, however, was the idea of an *infinite* universe that was in *constant motion*. Much of the *Atlas of the Underworld* is actually based on this notion of a universe in which everything including the waters and fire beneath Earth's surface is roiling in motion. That universe is also one in which mutation and change are a result of a constant reconfiguration of the four elements.

My father, a successful businessman who had to forego college to go to work at sixteen to support his widowed mother, was not the strictly sensate person I implied he was in the first paragraph of this article. Even though he was a Republican and took me to meet Nixon in the Senate when I was seven, he seems actually to have been a closet Marxist, unbeknownst to himself, in that his favorite diversion was to discover in his reading of old geographies the impact of geography and climate on demographic movements, and on economic conditions such as quality of life and education. It was from him that I learned of a kind of "contextualism," the fact that information is always skewed by the economic perspective and interests of the informer. He loved to point out distortions in medieval maps, and it was this view actually coupled with my mother's interest in grammatical syntax that seeded my own life-long preference for the *history* of ideas, that is for looking at an idea in its historical context, to looking at it in some discrete way independent of the rich and meaningful convolutions, reversals, and vagaries of its history.

This predilection for considering the context and the psychological determinants of an idea, and an openness to a semiotic perspective which would see the representation of those ideas as somehow encoding their psychological and social determinants, is for me analogous to Kircher's idea that in every expression of nature there is an encoding of mystic knowledge. Rowland speaks of the appearance (when Kircher was writing about the Pamphili Obelisk) of the Pythagorean figure of Harpocrates, the "infant god who raises his finger to his lips as an injunction to silence." For Pythagoras, as well as for Kircher, this figure signaled the idea that the surface meaning of something can at once conceal *and nurture* the hidden knowledge beneath (Rowland 2000, 15).

Thus it was in the perusal and study of this book that my relationship with my father was transformed. In the encounter with a book of my father's that he understood in a literal way as an incomplete but none-the-less objective record of natural science, while I understood it as a book with a subterranean undercurrent of mystic and alchemical knowledge, I felt that we could live in the same universe. Second, in musing over the personified image of the theory of correspondences that appears near the end of the *Atlas* (see opposite page), I discovered in the law of analogy and correspondences an antidote to what I felt was his literalism. The idea of correspondences, or analogy, seems to be not only the root source of metaphor, but key to awakening our collective potential as humans to *imagine* in a much needed more pluralistic way. This capacity to imagine seems for Kircher and Bruno to be embedded in the very structure of the cosmos. In time could my father have shared Kircher's idea that there a generative encoding of some originary knowledge in every level of nature's self expression?

BIBLIOGRAPHY

Coudert, Allison. 1980. *The Philosopher's Stone.* London: Wildwood House.

Findlen, Paula. ed., 2004. *Athanasius Kircher: The Last Man Who Knew Everything.* New York: Routledge.

Godwin, Jocelyn. 1979. *Athanasius Kircher (Art & Imagination),* London: Thames & Hudson, Ltd.

Gould, Stephen Jay. 2004. "Father Athanasius on the Isthmus of the Middle State; Understanding Kircher's Paleontology." *Athanasius Kircher: The Last Man Who Knew Everything.* Ed. Paula Findlen. New York: Routledge.

Kircher, Athanasius 1678. *d'Onderaardse Erde,* or *Mundus subterraneus [Atlas of the Underworld],* 2nd edition, Amsterdam: Joannem Janssonium à Waesberge & Filios.

Rowland, Ingrid. 2000. *The Ecstatic Journey: Athanasius Kircher in Baroque Rome.* Chicago: University of Chicago Library.

——, 2004. "Athanasius Kircher, Giordano Bruno, and the *Panspermia* of the Infinite Universe." *Athanasius Kircher: The Last Man Who Knew Everything.* Ed. Paula Findlen. New York: Routledge.

Van Leeuwen, Thomas A.P. Spring 2004. *The Underground World of Semi-Consciousness, in "The Magic Stove,"* a compendium of articles accompanying the Projective Theory seminar series with Thomas A.P. van Leeuwen. Netherlands: The Berlage Institute. www.berlage-institute.nl/03_postgraduate/Magic%20Stove/ms_art2.html.

Wilson, David, curator. 2000. *The World is Bound with Secret Knots: The Life and Work of Athanasius Kircher, 1602–1680.* Los Angeles, The Museum of Jurassic Technology. Ongoing exhibit.

ABSTRACT

DOROTHY NISSEN, "The Earth Is an Alembic; an 'imaginal' reading of the images in Athanasius Kircher's *Mundus subterraneus [Atlas of the Underworld]."* The article describes a transformative personal experience in growing up with a seventeenth century book that belonged to her father. [Athanasius Kircher (1662-1680), *Mundus subterraneus (Atlas of the Underworld), XII libros digestus,* Amsterdam, Janssonio-Waesbergiana, 1678.] JUNG JOURNAL: CULTURE & PSYCHE, 1:4, 18-31.

KEY WORDS

alchemy, "as above, so below," Athanasius Kircher, *Atlas of the Underworld,* awe, caves, *Mundus subterraneus, palingenesis,* seventeenth century worldview, spontaneous generation, theory of correspondences.

Painting by the Israeli Artist Orna Millo
(by permission of the artist)

JUNG JOURNAL: CULTURE & PSYCHE, FALL 2007, VOL. 1, NO. 4, 32-42

The (Non) Representation of Trauma: Analysis of Unnamed Painting by the Israeli Artist Orna Millo

HENRY AND ELLA ABRAMOVITCH

The Israeli artist Orna Millo has created an extraordinary and most disturbing painting. It was a centerpiece of her recent one-woman show at the Agripas 12 Gallery in Jerusalem (2006), and like all the other works, had no name. The namelessness of this painting is the first hint that we are entering dangerous psychic territory in which language and speech cannot guide us. For convenience's sake, we have chosen to title the painting with intentional paradox, *The (Non) Representation of Trauma*. We believe this painting is a unique psychological masterpiece depicting the psychic representation of trauma in visual form — and at the same time, the impossibility of representing trauma at all. Yet there is more. Uncannily, the painting draws the viewer *unheimlich* (literally "unhomelike") so the viewer becomes complicit in a scene that he or she cannot understand but nevertheless experiences as traumatizing.

The painting is visually very complex and difficult to take in because it is composed of six distinct picture planes. It is Orna Millo's virtuosity that allows her to stitch together these six distinct realms into a nightmarish whole. In addition to providing a title for the painting itself, we have given evocative names to the six picture planes:

HENRY ABRAMOVITCH is a Jungian analyst living in Jerusalem. He is a training analyst and past president of the Israel Institute of Jungian Psychology, member of the Ethics Committee of the International Association for Analytical Psychology (IAAP), and a former chair of the Israel Anthropological Association. His hobbies include sculpting and painting. *Correspondence:* 4 Tei Hai Street, Jerusalem, 92107 Israel. E-mail address: abramh@post.tau.il.

ELLA ABRAMOVITCH studied art and curatorship at the Israel Museum, where her life size photographs of four museum guards are part of the permanent exhibit in the Youth Wing. She is a freshman at Hebrew University of Jerusalem and is the eldest daughter of Henry Abramovitch.

- Green curving snakes
- Two figures staring out unable to speak
- Wheat field set against the darkening light
- Broken stage set giving an artificial flavor of the abyss
- Landscape at night
- The breakdown of form

We will discuss each picture plane in turn and only then try to comprehend the painting as a whole.

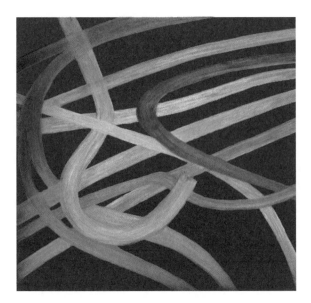

Green Curving Snakes

The first and most dominant layer of the painting is a swirling series of serpentine shapes in various shades of textured green that we will refer to as "snakes." A first glance gives an immediate double contrast, outwardly and inwardly. The curving sensuality of the "snakes" contrasts with the harsh rigidity of the outer rectangular picture frame; and at the same time, the overwhelming green clashes with the softer browns and pictorial forms in the inner space. Close inspection of the "snakes" reveals their sinuous texture; they seem both in motion and yet static, the first of many oppositions that come together in the painting. These "snakes" could well form an independent work of art.

Most works of art seek to draw the viewer into the realm depicted by the picture space. This is certainly true of the Impressionists, but even disturbing paintings such as Munch's *Scream* pull the observer in and trigger "mirror neurons" until it is all w can do not to clutch the sides of our faces and scream. With this painting, the opposite is true. The emotional impact of the snakes blocks the viewer's access to the world within, as if to say, "Stay back. Keep Away!" Here is the first element of the representation of trauma. The traumatic scene is isolated from external reality.

Once the trauma defense is organized, all relations with the outer world are "screened" by the self-care system. What was intended to be a defense against further trauma becomes a major resistance to all unguarded spontaneous expressions of self in the world. The person survives but cannot live creatively. (Kalsched 1995, 4)

The snakes represent the trauma defense, originally designed to protect the traumatized space from further wounding, but which ultimately serves to isolate and freeze the trauma in time. As Freud noted, there is no time in the unconscious; the traumatic experience is in the timeless, psychic tense of the present continuous. The snakes visually appear like a protective mesh, similar to the dark forest that surrounds the palace of Sleeping Beauty.

If we take a closer look at the "snakes," we can see ten lines that can be divided into a number of distinct groups. The first group consists of the six green lines of similar width and grace that move across the horizontal. All six "snakes" begin and end beyond the picture frame and appear with intense directional energy — even if it is not clear in which direction the "snakes" are moving. This visual ambiguity also reflects the duality of traumatized libido, which is glacier-like in its ability to move forward and backward at the same time — or in more psychological language, within the trauma zone, it is unclear what is regression and what is progression. Kalsched, in his now classic study, *The Inner World of Trauma*, describes this confusion of past and present:

> The primitive defense does not learn anything about realistic danger as the child grows up. It functions on the magical level of consciousness with the same level of awareness it had when the original trauma or traumas occurred. Each new life opportunity is mistakenly seen as a dangerous threat of re-traumatization and is therefore attacked. In this way, the archaic defenses become anti-life forces which Freud understandably thought of as part of the death instinct. (1995, 5)

Notice how much space and energy the "snakes" command. Within the psyche, these massive defensive structures leave little libido for anything else.

Besides the six horizontal "snakes," there are four more lines that traverse a more complex path. One "snake" on the right side of the painting is parabolic in its contour and curves back upon itself. Within the picture space, this parabolic snake surrounds the image of a boy, separating him from the female

image and the rest of the pictorial space. Inside the region defined by this snake, the boy is isolated; outside the region, the dark green of the parabola merges with the sky above and the abyss below.

Another distinctive line resembles an upside-down question mark. This is the only "snake" that ends within the picture, appearing abruptly torn or broken off while pointing directly to the boy's crotch — a further clue to the obscure nature of the trauma that somehow involves the boy's genitals and his sexuality. The snakes now have a sinister, sexualized sensuality. We will return to this point later.

At the same time, three lines meet to cover and hide his hands. If we understand that hands typically symbolize a person's ability to operate in the world, to get things done, then that function is impaired, or perhaps worse, totally annihilated. Three lines also converge on the female's face, leaving only a tiny bit of forehead and hair. The tone of this dramatic scene is that the female has experienced something of which she is not able to speak. Another line cuts across her arms and leaves one hand and only a few fingertips on the partly hidden hand. The depiction of the boy and female presents another set of polar opposites: The female has no face and no mouth, but a hand and some fingertips. The boy can see; however, it is not entirely clear whether or not he is able to speak. He has no hands available to him, but his feet are firmly planted on the ground, whereas the female's feet are obscured by the "snakes." Her ungrounded position corresponds with the phenomenology of trauma; victims feel they are always on unsolid ground.

Two Figures Staring Out Unable to Speak

Moving beyond the "snakes" to the figures, the female is so obscured it is hard to know whether she is a sister, playmate, babysitter, or mother. The green lines divide up each figure into small bits. She is composed of forehead and hair, left shoulder, right shoulder, triangle of abdomen, rectangle of skirt, a sliver of skirt, and triangle of two legs. The boy is made up of much bigger chunks: the head is connected to a long wavy area, and the thorax and shoulder are part of an even larger space and likewise the legs. The boy is thus composed of five large pieces, each of which is connected to the rest of the pictorial space, whereas the female figure is composed of seven small, even tiny, fragments that are unconnected to something collective — the archetypal whole. Here, too, Millo gives visual expression to the experience of fragmentation:

...when trauma strikes the developing psyche of a child, a fragmentation of consciousness occurs in which different "pieces" (Jung called them splinter-psyches or complexes) organize themselves according to certain archaic and typical (archetypical) patterns, most commonly dyads or syzygies made up of personified "beings"...In dreams, the regressed part of the personality is usually represented as a vulnerable, young, innocent (often feminine) *child- or animal-self* who remains shamefully hidden. (Kalsched 1995, 3)

Heinz Kohut called this phenomenon *disintegration anxiety,* an unnamable dread associated with the threatened dissolution of a coherent self (1977, 104).

"Never again," says our tyrannical caretaker, "will the traumatized personal spirit of this child suffer this badly! Never again will it be this helpless in face of cruel reality...before this happens I will disperse it into fragments [dissociation], or encapsulate it and soothe it with fantasy [schizoid withdrawal], or numb it with intoxicating substances [addiction], or persecute it to keep it from hoping for life in this world [depression]...In this way I will preserve what is left of this prematurely amputated childhood — of an innocence that has suffered too much too soon. (Kalsched 1995, 5. Square brackets and ellipsis in original.)

Although the two figures are not touching, they clearly form a pair. Their posture and composition recall the work of the American photographer, Diane Arbus. She was well known for her shots of "freaks," and in this context, she wrote:

Freaks was a thing I photographed a lot. It was one of the first things I photographed and it had a terrific excitement for me. I just used to adore them. I still do adore some of them. I don't quite mean they're my best friends but they made me feel a mixture of shame and awe. There's a quality of legend about freaks. Like a person in a fairy tale who stops you and demands that you answer a riddle. Most people go through life dreading they'll have a traumatic experience. Freaks were born with their trauma. They've already passed their test in life. They're aristocrats. (Israel and Arbus 1972, 3)

In many of her photographs, pairs stare out at the viewer in a haunting visage. The cover photo of the monograph *Diane Arbus* — of identically dressed twin girls — comes closest to the composition of Millo's painting. These young girls have the same rigid posture, staring out at the viewer conveying a voyeuristic sense of "shame and awe." Unlike the pair in Millo's painting, the twins in Arbus's work are standing shoulder-to-shoulder, creating an illusion that they are really fused, symbiotic Siamese twins. Yet, they, too, are not holding hands. In Millo's picture, the pair are linked by one rectangle that includes them both, as if there is some subtle *participation mystique* between the two figures. The boy stares out engaging the viewer, his face half in shadow, with exquisite poignancy.

Arbus's twins are dressed identically. In the painting, there are also visual hues that echo each other. The female's light blue blouse resonates with the boy's dark blue shorts. His white shirt stands in opposition to her bright orange-red skirt; together they are suggestive of purity and blood, respectively. Beneath each figure, we find their shadow. His shadow starts from his feet and organically follows the contours of his body. Her shadow resembles an ominous blob, unconnected to the body-ego. The juxtaposition of figure and shadow suggests that the female has an undifferentiated relation with her shadow and, therefore, is in ever-present danger of the dark side taking over the ego.

The light, coming from the extreme right, is a transitional light. Is it dawn or is it twilight? From an archetypal point of view, what is the difference between the two? Dawn represents hope, renewal, rebirth; twilight represents darkness, death, thanatos. The painting is cast in ambiguous light. To us, the haunting atmosphere does suggest the time is dusk, and the inevitable descent into the dark night of the soul.

The "snakes" and the figures make up the heart of the painting, but Orna Millo added four more scenes that surround the boy and the female figure.

Wheat Field Set Against the Darkening Light

The wheat field, at the top of the painting, is an agrarian scene of a long empty field with a house (or haystack) located in the far distance. The feeling tone is one of distance, loneliness, and isolation. The boy and female figure have come a long way, and they are out on their own. Their vulnerability recalls the Biblical situation of a rape occurring in the field, where there is no deliverer to hear the maiden's cries:

> But if (it is) in the field the man finds the spoken-for girl
> and the man strongly-seizes her and lay with her,
> then he is to die, the man who lay with her, he alone.
> But to the girl you are not to do anything,
> the girl did not (incur) sin (deserving) of death,
> for just as (the case of) the man who rises up against his neighbor
>   and murders his life,
> so is this matter;
> for in the open-field he found her;
> when the spoken-for girl cried out,
> there was no deliverer for her.

(Deuteronomy 22:27; Fox 1995, 953)

Did something horrendous happen in that field? The atmosphere of the painting conveys the sense that we both know and do not know what really happened; and if we do know, we must not speak of it. In either case, the long pastoral field with its link to the Great Mother and the fertility cycle of death and rebirth clashes with the frozen watchfulness and thanatos of the figures.

Broken Stage Set Giving an Artificial Flavor of the Abyss

The broken stage set is just to the right of the boy. In some respects, it is the most disturbing image of all. If the wheat field provides a seamless background

linking the figures to nature as the Great Earth Mother, the stage set calls everything we see into question and reveals that things are not at all what they seem. The field where the boy is standing is abruptly exposed to reveal a set of beams. It is as if the entire scene is some elaborate stage set and that what we see is actually a carefully managed illusion. The incongruity of the beams creates a sense that the entire set is manufactured, not real. The juxtaposition of the stage set and the figures in the field where no one can hear their cry suggests the psychic defense common to victims of sexual abuse. It is the pervasive sense that what happened is "not real" or is "made up" or "never happened." Again, this sense of self-doubt and derealization reflects the experience of many trauma victims who ask in disbelief, "How do I know I am not simply making it all up?"

At the same time, beneath the beams lies the nameless abyss. The same patients who fight their sense of unreality may also say they feel like they are falling in a dark bottomless well: there is no stopping, only endless falling. Their double reality of illusion and abyss condenses the dissociative experience. Part of them does not believe that what really happened, really did happen; another part is totally consumed by the "black hole" of the trauma experience.

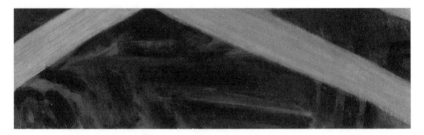

Landscape at Night

Placed on the bottom left is the "Landscape at Night." The details are difficult to discern, but the feel is of a mysterious but peaceful forest in the dark that may represent "the retreat to the forest" and with it the archetypal potential for healing and restoration. Its position below the two figures implies a connection with the unconscious and may have more sinister connections. It is the one part of the painting that provides visual relief.

Breakdown of Form

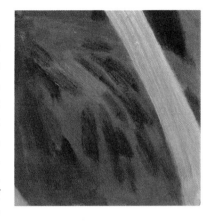

The Landscape at Night forms a pair with the last scene in the bottom-right region of the painting. Unlike the other areas, this one is not representational — however, it is not abstract either. Rather, it conveys a sense of the breakdown of form. Here, Millo points to the inability of form to contain the emotional intensity of the trauma state. In this regard, it may resemble "the more acute deprivations of infancy" described by Winnicott as "primitive agonies," the experience of which is "unthinkable" (1963, 90). This is the most primitive area of the soul in which experience is indigestible and remains incoherent and untold, lying beyond the limits of either visual or verbal representation.

The Painting as a Whole

A psychologically minded art historian wrote, "Unlike symptoms, which, one hopes, succumb to the power of good interpretation, great myths and works of art seem to thrive on interpretation. With it, they survive and flourish, and gain significance. Without it, they perish" (Spitz 1988, 377). The power of the painting lies in its suggestive quality, hinting at things unseen and able to grow through multiple interpretations. As a result, we are on dangerous ground when we try to translate the visual form into verbal discourse. And yet, to clarify the theme, we will suggest a tentative interpretation.

Some unknown trauma event occurred in the field. The trauma clearly has some erotic component as well as the forced silence of things we must not speak of. At this point, the narrative bifurcates. The boy and female might be split images of a single individual who has undergone the violation of innocence, the boy representing the observing ego and the female the lost, imprisoned, annihilated innocence. Alternatively, the trauma involves both of them. Deliberately, the painting does not tell what happened but forces us to enter in via our own active imagination. In either case, or in both cases, the rest of the painting shows how the psyche reacts to trauma by linking it to the healing forces of an Earth Mother, by making everything seem unreal, by entering the dark forest, and indeed when the center cannot hold, by form falling apart.

Most prominent is the psychic barrier of the "snakes" that signals to self and other that one is approaching a region of "unbearable psychic pain or anxiety" that needs to be denied, repressed, or dissociated. "For an experience to be 'unbearable' means that it overwhelms the usual defensive measures which Freud (1920, 27) described as a 'protective shield against stimuli'" (Kalsched 1995, 4). Nevertheless, the six picture planes that Millo's skill has melded into one show dissociation in action along with the danger of falling into the abyss and how trauma freezes its victims in time. Orna Millo has created a visual and psychological masterpiece that allows us to gaze deeply into the soul and see the (non) representation of trauma.

BIBLIOGRAPHY

Fox, Everett. 1995. *The Five Books of Moses: A New Translation with Introductions, Commentary and Notes.* New York: Schocken.

Freud, Sigmund. 1920. *Beyond the Pleasure Principle.* London: Hogarth Press.

Israel, Marvin and Doon Arbus. 1972. *Diane Arbus: Monograph.* New York: Aperture Monograph.

Kalsched, Donald. 1995. *The Inner World of Trauma.* London: Routledge.

Kohut, Heinz. 1977. *Restoration of the Self.* New York: International Universities Press.

Spitz, Ellen Handler. 1988. "The Inescapability of Tragedy," *Bulletin of the Menninger Clinic Foundation.* 52(2): 377–382.

Winnicott, Donald W. 1963. "The Fear of Breakdown" in *Psychoanalytic Explorations*, eds. C. Winnicott, R. Shepherd, and M. Davis, 87–95. Cambridge: Harvard University Press.

ABSTRACT

HENRY AND ELLA ABRAMOVITCH, "The (Non) Representation of Trauma: Analysis of Unnamed Painting by the Israeli Artist Orna Millo," JUNG JOURNAL: CULTURE & PSYCHE, 1:4, 32-42. This article discusses a nameless painting by the Israeli artist, Orna Millo, that the authors call "The (Non) Representation of Trauma." The painting depicts the psychic representation of trauma in visual form — and at the same time, the impossibility of representing trauma at all. The viewer is made complicit in a scene that he or she cannot understand but nevertheless experiences as traumatizing.

The painting is composed of six distinct picture planes, each of which characterizes a distinct aspect of traumatic experience as described by Kalsched. The six picture planes that Millo's skill has melded into one show dissociation in action along with danger of falling into the abyss and trauma freezing its victims in time. Orna Millo has created a visual and psychological masterpiece that allows us to gaze deeply into the soul and see the (non) representation of trauma.

KEY WORDS

trauma, child sexual trauma, repression, dissociation, abyss, Israel, forced silence, painting, Orna Millo, Diane Arbus, Donald Kalsched

JUNG JOURNAL: CULTURE & PSYCHE, FALL 2007, VOL. 1, No. 4, 43-68

Archetypal Patterns of Behavior:
A Jungian Analysis of the Mandala Structure
in the *Dialogues*
of Jean-Jacques Rousseau

GUILLEMETTE JOHNSTON

Critics have often suggested that Jean-Jacques Rousseau never managed to reconcile his favoring of spontaneous expression with his compulsive writing to explore his deepest feelings and thoughts. Indeed, it seems practically impossible for Rousseau himself to accept the obvious oppositions in his own philosophy, let alone his own psyche. Writing, for Rousseau, encourages a fundamental flaw — *amour-propre,* or pride, the main cause of division in mankind and in consciousness [1] — yet he himself adopted this craft, which for him a priori embodied everything but the genuine, transparent, and true. It should, therefore, not be surprising to find despair in *Rousseau Judge of Jean-Jacques: Dialogues,* [2] the fictitious yet autobiographical conversation Rousseau wrote late in life, when he frantically tries to convince the reader — and himself — of his good intentions with regard to, or in spite of, his involvement in writing. For Rousseau, the *Dialogues* served as a medium through which he could reach a new level of consciousness after encountering the depths of his unconscious. In its structure and meaning, the *Dialogues* illustrates the quest for the self (the totality of conscious and unconscious aspects of the

GUILLEMETTE JOHNSTON, who earned her Ph.D. in French at the University of California, Davis, is now a professor of Modern Languages at DePaul University, Chicago. A Rousseau specialist, she is currently exploring connections between Rousseau's spirituality, Jungian psychology, and kundalini yoga. She has been a member of the C.G. Jung Institute of Chicago and is now affiliated with the Jungian Society for Scholarly Studies. *Correspondence:* Department of Modern Languages, DePaul University, 802 West Belden Avenue, Chicago, Illinois 60614, USA.

person, including the ego) in terms of organizing principles that emphasize the natural transformation of one psychological attitude into another.

The aim of this study is to place the *Dialogues* of Jean-Jacques Rousseau within the global process of individuation as presented in analytical psychology. My argument is that Rousseau's *Dialogues* represents Rousseau's struggles with emerging unconscious content. Seen from this perspective, Rousseau's *Dialogues* illustrates an advanced stage in individuation, that is to say levels four and five,[3] corresponding on one hand to the withdrawal of ideological projections followed by the possibility of ego inflation, and on the other hand to the recognition of boundaries between the ego and the self through the internalization of psychic matter. The phenomenon of individuation not always being chronologically definable (any psychological development can present moments of regression or progression at each stage of its itinerary), my approach will consist of analyzing the structure of the *Dialogues* to show how this work fits into the pattern of the mandala.

Jung describes the mandala as an archetypal representation of "an inner image…gradually built up through (active) imagination…when psychic equilibrium is disturbed or when a thought cannot be found and must be sought for." Mandalas, which appear in all cultures but are perhaps best known through their use as representations of the cosmos in Tibetan Buddhism, "are all based on a quaternary system" (Jung, CW 12, ¶96) that in Tibetan mandalas appears as the square within the circle. For Jung, two attitudes (introversion/extraversion) and four function types (thinking, feeling, sensing, and intuiting) serve to measure the self-regulatory nature of the psyche. Thus, Jung adopted a form resembling the mandala when he identified the character types that describe the process of becoming conscious. The mandala serves to symbolize a process of transformation, a crossing between conscious and unconscious that provides the impetus for psychic growth.

The crisis Rousseau faced involved the merging of his introverted thinking with his extraverted feeling — a merging of conscious ego with unconscious content. This merging took place through the spontaneous creation of a mandala, a symbol of transformation. Because the *Dialogues* is one of a series of autobiographical works that mark crucial stages in Rousseau's quest for recognition and self-understanding, it is important to position this work within the context of Rousseau's life and writing, as well as to provide insight into Rousseau's understanding of his intentions in writing the *Dialogues* and his other works, before analyzing the mandala structure of the *Dialogues*. Therefore, this study will start with a biography of Rousseau and then give some background on the work to be analyzed. In addition, it will provide a summation of the *Dialogues* to put the analysis of this work in context and view Rousseau's writings from the perspective he provides in the *Dialogues,* positioning them within Rousseau's experience of individuation.

Jean-Jacques Rousseau: A Life

Jean-Jacques Rousseau was born in Geneva in 1712. His mother, who died of complications from his birth, left behind a library, and in his most famous autobiographical work, *The Confessions,* Rousseau describes how he and his father would read voraciously, often until dawn, to finish a book. Rousseau tells how at an early age "this dangerous method" — i.e., reading — "gave [him] an extraordinary facility in reading and understanding" as well as "an intelligence about the passions that was unique for [his] age" (1995, 7–8; 1959, 8). Rousseau's precociousness explains how, despite his unstable childhood and lack of formal education, he succeeded in writing works that have given him eternal posterity.

Abandoned by his father, who had to flee Geneva after a fight, Rousseau was taken in around age ten by the Calvinist pastor Lambercier and his sister. Rousseau recounts this period both as paradisiacal and as a time of disillusionment in which he first discovered injustice. Subsequently raised by an aunt, Rousseau felt like a second-rate member of the family. He was apprenticed to an engraver, and not being treated as an equal or as trustworthy in this position, he learned to steal and conceal. In 1728, coming back from a walk, Rousseau found the gates to Geneva closed, and resenting his apprenticeship, at age fifteen took up the life of a wanderer.

At the beginning of his wandering period, Rousseau met Mme de Warens, a convert to Catholicism who sent Rousseau to Turin to be baptized and renounce his Calvinism. Rousseau worked for a while for Mme de Vercelli and then for the Comte de Gouvon before abandoning a promising career with the Gouvon family and, after several adventures, returning to live with Mme de Warens in Chambery from 1732 to 1737 and in Les Charmettes, her retreat in the country close to Chambery, from 1737 to 1740. During his years with Mme de Warens, Rousseau furthered his education by reading voraciously, studying music, and exploring herbalism, among other things. In 1740, Rousseau left Les Charmettes, replaced in Mme de Warens' eyes by a new young lover. After a few months in Lyon as a tutor, Rousseau went to Paris (1741) to present a new system of musical notation to the Academy of Sciences. Failing to succeed with the Academy, Rousseau made the rounds of the Parisian salons, and in 1743, he became secretary to the French ambassador to Venice through the offices of Mme De Broglie, the daughter of a Polish-born baroness whom he had charmed (Cranston 1982, 160–161, 166). He soon fell out with the ambassador. Returning to Paris, in 1744 he collaborated with Voltaire on an opera and later wrote articles on music for the *Encyclopedia or Systematic Dictionary of the Sciences, the Arts, and the Professions,* co-founded by Denis Diderot and Jean d'Alembert. In 1746, he became secretary to Mme Dupin. Though he was received in Parisian society, he felt like a misfit. The fictitious character St. Preux in Rousseau's romantic novel *The New Heloise* describes the artificiality of Parisian social life.

It is important to know that Rousseau became known as a writer only with the success of the *Discourse on the Sciences and the Arts* (also called the *First Discourse*) in 1749, when he was in his late thirties. This work marks an important turning point in Rousseau's life. From the time of its publication until 1762, Rousseau wrote abundantly, each time maintaining that he was trying to put into writing the epiphany he had had on a summer afternoon in 1749 while traveling to visit his friend Denis Diderot at the prison of Vincennes. According to Rousseau, on his way to Vincennes, he read in the *Mercure de France* a question offering a literary prize: "Whether the reestablishment of the sciences and the arts contributed to purify the mores." Rousseau's crucial thesis was that man is naturally good and that society and civilization contribute to his corruption. (Speculations have been made as to the real source of Rousseau's inspiration, and it has been said that it was Diderot who encouraged Rousseau to put forward this brilliant paradox.)

In 1750, Rousseau published the *First Discourse,* won the prize, and became famous overnight. However, by putting into question the central assumptions and values of the Age of Reason, Rousseau placed himself in opposition to the dominant current of thought and found a formidable enemy in Voltaire, the guiding light of the spirit of Enlightenment. Soon after the success of the *First Discourse,* Rousseau gave up writing for the theatre and the opera to dedicate his life to philosophical reflection while copying music for a living. In 1754, Rousseau was again inspired to write a discourse when the Dijon academicians presented the question, "What is the origin of inequality among men, and is it authorized by natural law?" In his *Discourse on the Origins and Foundations of Inequality* (or the *Second Discourse*), Rousseau specifically criticizes the corruption of humanity by society and puts into question the rights of property as well as all laws and political systems that favor and protect the rich. Politics and social injustice are, according to Rousseau, fundamentally linked. This discourse further separated Rousseau from the Enlightenment philosophers, who, for the most part, were less involved in social criticism. This *Second Discourse* can also be construed as an "archeological" endeavor to understand the nature of humanity.

Two of the chief concepts in Rousseau's philosophy first come into prominence here and involve the notions of *amour-propre* and *amour de soi*. According to Rousseau, the fall of humankind results from a shift away from existence within *amour de soi,* which resembles a state of *participation mystique,* a condition of unity in which man feels at one with himself and nature. With the development of society, this self-love that encourages compassion and recognition of the other deviates into pride or *amour-propre*. Shame and pride are born out of the fact that humans start reflecting about their condition compared to that of their neighbors. The *Second Discourse* did not win the Dijon prize, and Rousseau left Paris for Geneva and abjured his Catholic faith, reconverting to Calvinism.

In 1756, Rousseau went back to France, accepting an invitation to live in Montmorency at L'Ermitage on the property of Mme d'Epinay, against the advice of his friend Diderot. Though he enjoyed his time at the retreat, a series of disturbances, including gossip generated by Thérèse Levasseur's mother,[4] interference from Diderot, a passion for Mme d'Houdetot (the inspiration for the character Julie in Rousseau's *New Heloise*) despite her involvement with the poet St. Lambert, and manipulations by Diderot's friend Grimm, turned Mme d'Epinay against Rousseau. In 1757, Rousseau left L'Ermitage and fell out with Diderot for good. He wrote a letter to Jean d'Alembert condemning the establishment of a theatre in Geneva, arguing that it would contribute to the corruption of an otherwise moral people. This letter furthered the rift between Rousseau and other philosophers, specifically d'Alembert and other Encyclopedists and above all Voltaire, a devotee of the theatre. Rousseau thereafter isolated himself in a small house in Montmorency (Mont Louis, 1758–1762) and wrote three of his most important works, *The New Heloise, The Social Contract,* and *Emile,* in an intense period of creativity. A few days after *Emile* was published in 1762, the Parliament in Paris confiscated the work and had it burned, claiming that the profession of faith by the Savoyard vicar in the book was blasphemous. Rousseau fled to Switzerland from France to avoid arrest, but in Geneva *Emile* and *The Social Contract* were burned and a warrant was issued for his arrest, so he could not return to his native city. Expelled also from Bern, he took refuge in Yverdon and then in Môtiers. These banishments and Rousseau's quarrels with his friends contributed to the exacerbation of Rousseau's paranoia in later years.

In the last sixteen years of his life (1762–1778), Rousseau's writing concentrated on a series of autobiographical works and on personal correspondence, all of which can be viewed as attempts to justify himself in the eyes of the world. One can highlight several types of writings during this period. During his three years in Môtiers (1762–1765), Rousseau wrote to Christophe de Beaumont, archbishop of Paris, responding to censures against *Emile.* He also wrote nine letters, known as *Letters Written from the Mountains* (1764), defending *The Social Contract* and asking his supporters to protest the decisions of the Council of Geneva. Additionally, as early as 1761 Rousseau's editor had asked him to write his autobiography. An anonymous brochure published in 1764 had denounced his attitude toward religion and criticized aspects of his life. These facts incited Rousseau to write his memoirs to justify himself to posterity. Rousseau wrote the first six books of this work, *The Confessions,* from March 1765 to August 1767. Books VII to XII were composed from 1769 to 1770. After a pamphlet, "The Sentiment of the Citizens," possibly written by Voltaire, stirred public opinion against Rousseau in 1765 by announcing that he had abandoned his children, Rousseau's house in Môtiers was attacked, and he fled to the island of St. Pierre in the Lac de Bienne, Canton of Bern, Switzerland. The idyllic time he spent there, later described in his *Reveries of the Solitary Walker,* ended when he was expelled by the Senate of Bern. Rousseau left for England, invited there by David Hume, but he fell out with Hume and returned to France in 1767. After several moves, he settled in Paris in 1770. From 1770 to 1778, Rousseau lived in the rue Plâtrière, nowadays known as rue Jean-Jacques Rousseau.

Rousseau thought of himself as the victim of a universal conspiracy. Though he undoubtedly was paranoid, in his later life Rousseau had numerous enemies, such as the Encyclopedists and some Catholics and Protestants. He had been attacked by mobs, and several governmental bodies had banned, censured, and even burned his works, and banished him or issued orders for his arrest. His paranoia was exacerbated by his quarrels with Grimm, Diderot, and Mme d'Epinay, and was heightened even more by his trip to England, during which he admixed fact and fantasy in his perception that Hume was conspiring against him (1766). His fears might have appeared justified to him later, when Hume published his correspondence with Rousseau to expose Rousseau's accusations. It was just after these events, in 1772–1776, that Rousseau wrote the three *Dialogues: Rousseau Judge of Jean-Jacques.* In this work, two characters, a Frenchman and "Rousseau," exchange perspectives on the character "Jean-Jacques" or "J.J." to determine if he is a malicious plagiarist and end up acknowledging his innocence. Rousseau tried to gain the trust of public opinion by distributing a prospectus on the street, entitled "To All Frenchmen Who Still Love Truth and Justice," summarizing his justifications. The public did not respond to this plea. After 1776, Rousseau gave up trying to justify himself, thinking that he would not be able to change the course of events. He wrote *The Reveries of the Solitary Walker* in the last two years of his life, a series of meditative autobiographical sketches that he composed for his own satisfaction. He died before he could complete the "Tenth Promenade" of this work.

The *Dialogues* and the Problem of Autobiography

Jean-Jacques Rousseau's autobiographical fiction, the *Dialogues,* presents ideal material to study the process of individuation. If placed in the context of all Rousseau's autobiographical works, we can see that it is conceived at the peak of a crisis, and that conversely to the preceding autobiographical work, *The Confessions,* it does not present a rational and realistic account of his life. Rather than retelling a series of events, the work consists of a fictional conversation inspired by actual occurrences (in other words, the banishment of Rousseau's work and Rousseau's falling out with his friends) and by Rousseau's feelings at the time he decided to write the *Dialogues.* We must remember Rousseau was prompted to start writing autobiographical works not by a desire for self-discovery, but by a desire to be understood and vindicated. The urge toward self-discovery was a byproduct that developed as the autobiographical works progressed (Cranston 1997, 180; Rousseau 1995, xviii, xxii).

Jean Starobinski, a leading Rousseau scholar, writes that for Rousseau, self-knowledge stems from intuitive knowledge. To the question "Who am I?" Rousseau answers, "I feel my heart" (Starobinski 1971, 216–223)—hence, the ever-changing content of Rousseau's autobiographical works, which call for the constant, renewable account of "the act of the sentiment." According to Rousseau, feelings are dependable signs that we must acknowledge and use in the introspective process. Thus the act of writing contributes to the endeavor to restore the self to the other by means of a multiplicity of points of view, which, thanks to a very detailed presentation of varied circumstances, present a reliable account that enables the reader to capture the essence of the very being of Rousseau.

Looking at the crucial moments in Rousseau's writing career, we can highlight two types of writing. One, we see the political, sociological, philosophical, and educational writings, which all have at base Rousseau's systematic questioning of the benefits of civilization, e.g., the arts and sciences when they cause us to forget the primordial, natural qualities of unity promoted by man's natural inclination toward compassion. This feeling also referred to as *pitié* or pity is the extension of *amour de soi* to the other. Second, Rousseau's autobiographical writings, *The Confessions,* the *Dialogues,* the *Reveries,* and other works, mark Rousseau's attempts to justify himself to those whose philosophical positions he had publicly questioned in his non-autobiographical writings. Rousseau is faced with the paradox of having to explain why, though he is denouncing the *esprit philosophique,* he himself uses writing—an art or even an artifice—to be understood. As Starobinski has mentioned, however, writing autobiographies serves Rousseau not as a quest for the remembrance of facts and things past, but as a process of discovering the self via the disclosure of feelings. We know that Rousseau started *The Confessions* in order to clear his name, whereas he wrote the *Dialogues* in a state of quasi-delirium at the time when he had been banished from many countries and rejected by many friends. It is the reality of the feelings of dejection and the desire to appeal for clarification and justice that prompted Rousseau to write the *Dialogues,* through which the reader can reconstruct the several stages of Rousseau's writing career.

The Structure and Plot of the *Dialogues*

The *Dialogues* is presented as a conversation between two characters, "Rousseau" (hereafter called "Rousseau Judge") and "The Frenchman." Although the central topic of discussion is "J.J." (short for "Jean-Jacques"), the discussion also concerns "The League," a quasi-imagined, quasi-real group of unspecified persons who have accused J.J. of being malicious, evil, and a plagiarist.[5] Hence, the work actually presents four voices: the League and J.J., who are absent, and Rousseau Judge and the Frenchman, who are present. It poses as primary characters an introverted thinking type (Rousseau Judge) and his opposite (the Frenchman), an extraverted feeling type who displays negative extraverted qualities. As the *Dialogues* progresses, though, the Frenchman becomes more like the Judge.

The first *Dialogue* opens with Rousseau Judge's description of an imaginary "parallel world" in which people live lives essentially shaped by self-love, *amour de soi,* and contentment, turning inward rather than outward in *amour-propre* or destructive, competitive pride. Rousseau

Judge reveals that he has found a reflection of this world in the writings of J.J., and that as an inhabitant of this parallel universe, he recognizes in J.J. a kindred soul. Meanwhile, the Frenchman insists that J.J. is a monster, a criminal, and a plagiarist. The two debate the authenticity of J.J.'s writings on music, and Rousseau Judge asks whether there might actually be two J.J.'s, one the author of the books describing the parallel world and the other the malicious "author" of the crimes attributed to him. The Frenchman describes the League's conspiracy against J.J., through which J.J. is never confronted, is thoroughly manipulated, and is never even made aware of his crimes. The Frenchman also reveals that he himself has never read J.J.'s works, having concluded that J.J. must be a monster because his reputation has been so thoroughly tarnished. Rousseau Judge argues against the Frenchman's belief that accusations are sufficient to prove guilt, basing his argument on principles of justice, and questions the validity of the League's maligning of J.J.'s character. The Frenchman states that if he were to find out that he were wrong in his judgment of J.J. he would hate J.J. even more on account of his error. Rousseau Judge and the Frenchman part, the Judge having decided to go observe J.J. directly and the Frenchman intent on reading J.J.'s works.

The two meet again at the beginning of the second *Dialogue.* Much of this dialogue is devoted to Rousseau Judge's description of J.J. The Judge reports that although J.J. is not "virtuous," he is not a monster. In fact, he is basically the same person he was before he started writing books and gained celebrity in his later life. Rousseau Judge describes his strategies in observing J.J., and he says that J.J. is not like the person he is widely imagined to be. He describes J.J. as inept at speech but spontaneous in the expression of truth — in other words, as someone who displays extremes of slothfulness and passionate activity and discussion. Rousseau Judge and the Frenchman discuss J.J.'s sensitivity, and Rousseau Judge states, "There never existed a being more sensitive to emotion and less formed for action" (1990, 117; 1959, 812). J.J. is a person prone to withdrawal into flights of imagination, like a "meditative Oriental."[6] The two discuss various portraits of J.J., including a popular one characterized as "the Cyclops," and Rousseau Judge describes Hume's role in promulgating this image. They then digress into a discussion on the effects of seeing something directly rather than through the eyes of others. Rousseau Judge reveals that J.J. thinks that he has been the victim of a conspiracy, of which the portraits are a part. The two discuss J.J.'s return to Paris, his sense of the falsity of Parisian society, and his withdrawal from Parisian society. The Frenchman expresses concern over the effects of beneficence toward a scoundrel, and Rousseau Judge admits the possibility of being deluded in judging others. They discuss Diderot's comment that "Only the wicked person...is alone" (1990, 99; 1959, 789), which is interpreted as an attack on J.J. (Cranston 1991, 47–54; Villaverde 1995, 5, 33–47). The discussion veers into *amour-propre,* which is described as the principle of wickedness and as inclining people to attribute to others qualities and motivations they themselves have. When the Frenchman asks how everyone can be so mistaken about J.J., Rousseau Judge replies that the will can influence judgment, and the two discuss "epidemics of the mind" and how the public can fall victim to "contagion" through manipulation (1990, 170; 1959, 880). J.J.'s attacks on the social order in his books have been interpreted as attacks on individuals. The League's strategy of disguising malevolence as benevolence is discussed. The two part, with the Frenchman vowing to read J.J.'s books.

The third *Dialogue* occurs several months later, when the Frenchman returns from the country. He has now read J.J.'s books, and has copied out several passages that illustrate J.J.'s attacks on society and on various social groups. Rousseau Judge does not deny that people should be angry about these attacks, but he maintains that they should reproach J.J.'s style, rather than engage in defamation. J.J. has written out of emotion driven by a moment of vision, not as a professional hack or "book factory," and this explains his occasional overzealousness in expression. The Frenchman claims that he still dislikes J.J., but now says he also disapproves of the tactics of those who malign J.J. He describes the conspiracy against J.J. as generated by J.J.'s comments against men of letters, and he now becomes the voice of restraint as Rousseau Judge calls for a vigorous defense of J.J. The two end up agreeing to work together to save his memory.

Individuation and Rousseau's Other Writings in the Context of the *Dialogues*

One of Rousseau's central concerns in writing the *Dialogues* is to assess the personal significance of his own literary development. He does this by describing his literary career and evaluating his works, which in the *Dialogues* he attributes to J.J. If we try to situate Rousseau's pertinent texts in accordance with the actual process of individuation, we distinguish several descriptive passages marking steps in the progression of his psychic evolution. The crucial initiatory moment of transformation takes place during the revelation at Vincennes, after which Rousseau chooses to write his *First Discourse.* In the *Dialogues,* the fictitious character Rousseau Judge discerns this rupture and transition in the life of the accused J.J. Addressing himself to the Frenchman, he declares

> You must admit that this man's destiny has some striking peculiarities. His life is divided into two parts that seem to belong to two different individuals, with the period that separates them — meaning the time when he published books — marking the death of one and the birth of the other. (1990, 14; 1959, 676)

Later on, after having paid a visit to J.J., Rousseau Judge will alleviate his doubt while reporting on the ominous fate of J.J. the author:

> He attained and passed maturity without dreaming of writing books, and without feeling for a moment the need for that fatal celebrity.... It was even, in a way, by surprise and without making a plan that he found himself thrust into that fatal career.... An unfortunate question from the Academy that he read in the Mercure suddenly... showed him another universe, a true golden age... and fulfilled in hopes all his visions.... From the lively effervescence that developed then in his soul came those sparks of genius that have glittered in his writings during ten years of delirium and fever....[7]

This vision determined the career of the real Rousseau as an author. It corresponds to the encounter of the conscious with the unconscious, the putting of the two psychic systems into symbolic contact. The vision at Vincennes and its consequences in the broader sense are the conscious beginning of individuation, which after all can occur with only a certain degree of lucidity on the part of the individual (Rousseau 1995, 83–86; 1959, 104–110). Seen with regard to individuation's temporal trajectory, this moment corresponds to the third level of psychic development, when the individual, following a vision, establishes his values, now modified, at the level of abstraction. As Rousseau puts it in *The Confessions,* throughout this time he was "intoxicated with virtue" to the point of being "truly transformed" (1995, 350).

The writing of *The Confessions* itself presents another major moment in Rousseau's psychological growth. In fact, in the *Dialogues* Rousseau Judge intuitively recognizes the creation of *The Confessions* as a crucial step in the internal configuration of the self, and he also recognizes the unexpected external consequences of this configuration:

> This reading which he lavished on so many people, but of which so few were capable... gave him the courage to say everything, and to treat himself with a justice that is often even too rigorous. When he saw himself distorted among men to the point of being considered

a monster, conscience — which made him feel more good than bad in himself — gave him the courage that perhaps he alone had and will ever have to show himself as he was. (1990, 188; 1959, 902–903)

This double gesture of introspection and exhibition marks a transgression with regard to the public relations that Rousseau had had until then. The modification of his character, the act of conscience that "made him feel more good than bad in himself," reveals a pressing desire for self-recognition, a need to define and unify himself — a characteristic proper to the first phase of the process of individuation, that is, the unification of the ego complex. *The Confessions,* through its expression of a desire for clarification, symbolizes the crystallization of the ego complex.

The Confessions remains one of the most subjective, interpretative, and concentrated works with regard to both the author's perception and the work's public reception. Still, the reader cannot deny the quest for unity expressed in its writing, as J.J.'s repeated if not obsessive worry to warn us about possibly confusing the two expressions of *amour-propre* and *amour de soi* suggests. On the other hand, *The New Heloise* involves conscious elaboration of a waking dream, an imaginary world in which Rousseau creates a community living in a system that follows his heart; and this work can be placed at levels three, four, and sometimes five of individuation. *The New Heloise* combines, in fact, characteristics of an abstraction of values or a creation of an ideology with an awareness both of the relativity of values and of the boundaries separating the ego and unconscious forces. *Heloise* does not fool Rousseau Judge, since he recognizes in the work the elaboration of an ideal of love that leads eager female readers to invest J.J. with qualities that will lead to disappointment. The Judge explains the misunderstanding produced by the idealism of *The New Heloise* as follows:

> *The Heloise* had turned the glances of women to him. They had rather natural rights to a man who described love in that way. But knowing hardly anything about it except the physical side, they believed that only very lively senses could inspire such tender feelings, which might have given them a higher opinion of the person expressing them than he perhaps deserved. (1990, 189; 1959, 903–904)

If the idealized universe of *The New Heloise* incited female readers to exaggerated projections of absolute values onto its author, this work remains nonetheless a landmark in the unification of Rousseau's internal world. *Emile* also fits in with these three levels. It expresses the unity of this project by offering a solution via the psychic development of the child and of Rousseau, who in moments of crisis, finds comfort in its text. Describing a paroxysm of despair, Rousseau writes, "[a] passage of *Emile* that I recalled made me return within myself and find what I had vainly sought outside" (1990, 252; 1959, 985). I do not include Rousseau's *Reveries* among these written symbols of psychic maturation because this book was written after the *Dialogues.*

The Mandala in the *Dialogues* of Jean-Jacques Rousseau

By *individuation* Jung implied a coming to terms with oppositions within the psyche, including oppositions that cross the boundaries of the conscious and the unconscious. In Rousseau's case, we can speak of these oppositions as involving the "rational author" and the "sensitive man." The *Dialogues* thus can be said to illustrate archetypal patterns and behaviors that we can study according to principles enunciated by Jung. To show how Rousseau's text brings satisfactory closure to a problem of irreconcilable oppositions in his consciousness, I will highlight the mandala structure of the *Dialogues,* suggesting how behaviors and writings that seem inconsistent do, in fact, demonstrate processes that integrate diverse functions associated with the different character types, and I will argue that this synthesis contributes to reestablishing peace, balance, and wholeness within him. To do this, I will analyze the characters according to definite functions, to show how, when seen as a whole, they can represent the integration of multiple sides in the psyche of Rousseau the author. The two aspects of introverted thinking and extraverted feeling, as polarized functions, represent the reflective qualities of the introverted writer and the open, sharing side of the publicly renowned author. In each case, these opposing functions are presented both directly and in a "shadow" model that illustrates opposing tendencies within the functions themselves that call for compensation.

Jung's model of the psyche involves interaction among the four functions of thinking, feeling, sensing, and intuiting, yet because we cannot use all four at once, we develop a primary function that inevitably excludes its opposing function from consciousness. The opposing or inferior function in the quaternary system is the least developed and hence the most difficult one for the individual to cope with. As an example, a person with a developed (conscious) thinking function theoretically would have difficulty coping with the (largely unconscious) feeling function. The two other functions become isolated as auxiliary functions. If the primary function is introverted thinking, the inferior function is extraverted feeling, and the extraverted feeling tends to interfere with the thinking function. The auxiliary functions, sensing and intuiting, do not conflict with the primary function.

A key component of Jungian theory is its system of polarity or opposition. Inspired by Heraclitus's enantiodromia, this system sees life as "made up everywhere of pairs of opposites ... at once irreconcilable as well as inseparable.... [T]he 'poles' of the opposites are best perceived as moving through a natural process of transformation and change of one into the other" (Spoto 1995, 36). To highlight the prime organizing principle of this "law of compensation," Jung writes

> The activity of consciousness is selective. Selection demands direction. But direction requires the exclusion of everything irrelevant. This is bound to make the conscious orientation [q.v.] one-sided. The contents that are excluded and inhibited by the chosen direction sink into the unconscious, where they form a counterweight to the conscious orientation. The strengthening of this counter position keeps pace with the increase of conscious one-sidedness until finally a noticeable tension is produced.... The more one-sided the conscious attitude, the more antagonistic are the contents arising from the unconscious, so that we may speak of a real opposition between the two.... As a rule, the unconscious compensation does not run counter to consciousness, but is rather a balancing or supplementing of the conscious orientation.... Normally, compensation is an unconscious process, i.e., an unconscious regulation of conscious activity. In neurosis the unconscious appears in such stark contrast to the conscious state that compensation is disturbed. The aim of analytical therapy, therefore, is the realization of unconscious contents in order that compensation may be re-established. (Jung, CW 6, ¶¶419–420; Spoto 1995, 36–37)

The dynamic involved in compensation, as described here, is apparent throughout Rousseau's *Dialogues*. Besides attempting to adapt to his inner world and to the world around him, Rousseau is dealing in the *Dialogues* with the two functional aspects linked to authorship. If we can summarize Rousseau's disarray in terms of grievances (witch hunting by the League), we can also summarize his ploy in terms of the creation and justification of the self through an understanding of authorship that reconciles attitudes of introversion and extraversion as well as the opposition between the functions of thinking and feeling.

A famous author must often learn to balance the status of the introverted thinker who uses qualities necessary for composition with that of the extraverted feeler who can reach the other and relate smoothly with the outside world. Authorship seen in this light involves having to face acknowledgment, and this means knowing how to shift introverted energies into extraversion to facilitate reception of the work and its creator. This ability becomes especially important when the author, like Rousseau, denies any distance between himself and the moral and intellectual content of his writing.

Being famous as a writer was problematic for Rousseau as long as these two sides refused to integrate with one another. This type of dilemma often involves an ego wishing to overlook its hidden side, or in Jungian terms, its shadow — those "unknown or little-known attributes and qualities of the ego ... that mostly belong to the personal sphere."[8] Jung's description of the shadow accurately conveys the scenario Rousseau faced. The Heraclitean "irreconcilable" yet "inseparable" qualities that favor transformation of one side of the self into the other might not suit the hidden agenda of the ego, which is autocratically inclined to wish to remain in charge of conscious operations. Ego defines its individuality by its separateness from the greater, generally unconscious components of the self, and it likes to assume that it has control over unconscious content. For Jung, in individuation, the ego surrenders its perception of supremacy in the psychic system in order to allow new energies to be brought in from the inferior side.

The *Dialogues* presents many traits and qualities that are typical of a symbol of transformation as represented in Jungian psychology. Rousseau concocted this work on an urge, paradoxically "despite" himself, out of his tortured imagination, reflecting the point that "Man ... produces symbols unconsciously and spontaneously" (Jung 1964, 21). Further, because basically four voices are represented in the *Dialogues* (two present: Rousseau Judge and the Frenchman, and two absent: the League and J.J.), we can identify within the *Dialogues* a structure recalling the mandala: a quaternary representation of an inner struggle that constitutes a quest for recognition of and balance between conscious and unconscious forces through active imagination at a time of crisis. If we consider the different levels at work in the creation of symbols of transformation, we can approach the *Dialogues* from two angles: via the creative process that generated it and via the forces this process aimed to integrate. This approach will lead to examining different aspects of the shadow that present the difficulties involved in integration. These difficulties appear in the discussion of choosing authorship as a career and so adopting the flaws of this profession, in the accusations and denunciations directed at the

League and in the justification of J. J.'s temperament. Such manifestations of the shadow—of the author Rousseau's hidden personality and agenda—symbolize the elements that Rousseau needed to recognize and integrate into his psyche.

Writing the *Dialogues* did not, according to Rousseau, follow his typical practice. Desperation rather than a wish to inform his audience led him on this path. The character Rousseau Judge in the *Dialogues* makes this point clear. Justifying J. J.'s behavior to the Frenchman, he declares

> Finally, despite the resolution he had made when he arrived in Paris not to write any more about this subject [i.e., himself]…he made one more effort, and attending once again to his destiny and to his persecutors despite himself, he wrote a kind of judgment of them and of himself in the form of a Dialogue, rather like the one that may result from our conversations.…[H]e rarely spent more than a quarter of an hour on it each day, and that choppy and interrupted manner of writing is one of the causes of the lack of continuity and continual repetitions that prevail in this writing. (1990, 136–137; 1959, 836–837)

This passage suggests that, with regards to its composition, the *Dialogues* was more of an unconscious than a conscious creation. Rousseau Judge reports that in spite of himself, at sporadic intervals, J. J. took up writing his *Dialogues,* which indeed seem repetitive, incoherent, and tormented.

The definite, doubled oppositions that mark the beginning of the *Dialogues* are made clear through the presence of the characters who represent the opposition between J. J. and the League. Perhaps it is not by chance that we recognize distinct, opposing attitude types in the characters of the Frenchman and Rousseau Judge. In a precise manner, the Judge can point out the lack of logic in the reasons laid out by J. J.'s opponents, thereby leading us to see him as an introverted thinker, as when he tries to deduce if J. J. is actually the author of the books attributed to him:

> …whatever is the case about the true Author of the piece [The Village Soothsayer], that the person who claims to be the author cannot have been in a position to have written it due to his ignorance and his inability is enough for me to conclude even more strongly that he did not write the Dictionary he also claims, or the Letter on French Music, or any of the other books…and that it is impossible not to feel that they all come from the same hand. (1990, 21; 1959, 685–686)

By contrast, the Frenchman, in his quick, judgmental way, appears as an extraverted feeler because he superficially but vehemently repeats public opinion rather than offering his own conclusions. Answering Rousseau Judge, who has concluded that the person who wrote *The Village Soothsayer* could not have also written the *Dictionary of Music,* the Frenchman says, "Knowing neither of these works, I cannot judge your reasoning by myself. I only know that the assessment of the public about this is totally different" (1990, 18; 1959, 681).

The behavior that the real Rousseau, the author of the *Dialogues,* attributes to the Frenchman is not simply extraverted feeling, but extraverted feeling that has gotten out of hand. Far from conveying such positive extraverted qualities as empathy, willingness to help, candor, and optimism (Meier 1989, 73), the Frenchman displays negative feeling-function tendencies such as tactlessness, indiscretion, thoughtlessness, extravagance in judgment, and recklessness — manifestations of a poorly developed and unintegrated inferior function. Indeed, despite his own acknowledged ignorance regarding J.J.'s integrity or innocence, the Frenchman does not hesitate to perpetuate gossip about J.J. and thus even takes part in the conspiracy of lies and defamation. The Frenchman reminds the Judge of the agreement not to reveal anything that the Frenchman has told him concerning J.J. and also gives the Judge malicious advice so the Judge himself can join the evil conspiracy: "Your commitment, which you cannot fail to keep without breaking your word, has no shorter duration than your lifetime.... [Y]ou must work in concert with everyone to keep him always in ignorance of what is known and of how it is known."[9]

If the Frenchman appears despicable, Rousseau the author does sometimes give him a bluntness and honesty reminiscent of J.J. as the latter is seen by the Judge. At the onset of the investigation, the Frenchman admits that it will be hard for him to forgive J.J. if he is innocent because his innocence will reveal the Frenchman's guilt: "I feel that while respecting him and doing him justice, I would then hate him more, perhaps, for my errors than I hate him now for his crimes. I would never forgive him for my injustice toward him" (1990, 78–79; 1959, 761). This positive streak enables the Frenchman to become more like Rousseau Judge as the *Dialogues* progresses. In the third *Dialogue,* the Frenchman offers the Judge his own insightful and redeeming report on J.J., displaying the sound qualities of an introverted thinker (Rousseau 1990, 207–211; 1959, 927–933). Here, the Frenchman comes to represent negative because unconscious and unadapted sides of the self that have been faced, reconsidered, and reintegrated into the psyche. The Frenchman's conversion to J.J.'s cause suggests reconciliation with the other side as well as an initial opening toward compassion. If the Frenchman is only a fictitious adversary who the author Rousseau created, giving this adversary positive qualities is a way to see the other in a more positive light and consequently to accept, at some level, his own negative sides. The Frenchman's revealing words concerning his previous denial underline these affinities shared by the originally opposed sides: "I never wished to approach their prey to … deceive … following their example, and the same repugnance I saw in your heart was in mine when I sought to fight it" (1990, 217; 1959, 940).

While the exchange between Rousseau Judge and the Frenchman allows for an opening of the heart and for compromise to redeem J.J., a closer look at the issues at stake in this battle helps explain the author Rousseau's ordeal more clearly. By presenting opposite sides of the quaternity both directly and indirectly (since J.J.'s opinions are reported only through the Judge), Rousseau has chosen to have the Judge, in J.J.'s defense, lay out his — Rousseau the author's — grievances regarding the profession of author as well as his criticisms of the League. The League, source of all conspiracies against J.J., becomes symbolic of the base profession of letters. The descriptions Rousseau Judge and J.J. give of the literary world disclose the negative aspects of introverted thinking involved in the writing profession. The portrayal of the behavior of the literati reveals a marked neurosis that is a direct result of adopting a counter-position whose compensatory effects have been disturbed, thereby destroying normal processes of compensation aimed at balancing different elements of the psyche.

Once drawn into the unconscious, far from exhibiting wholeness in coping with the necessary regulating interactions between the poles of opposites (introverted thinker and extraverted feeler), the conscious qualities of the introverted thinking side are pushed to the extreme and appear to be taken over by the unconscious, extraverted feeling side. This side itself, by its very unconsciousness, is out of control. Looking at introverted qualities (e.g., discernment), which turn into extraverted qualities such as overbearingly acute critical senses and tendencies toward paranoia and insecurity, we can see how, in attempting to achieve control, the side representing the literary profession, mesmerized by the other side as embodied in the outside world, falls into an opposing extreme. It now becomes bound to the extraverted feeling realm and so brings together the most unsavory qualities of each side.

Where positive introverted qualities of nuance, insight, and consideration lay, coldness, defiance, and haughtiness have taken over, turning the spectrum toward negative extraverted qualities such as ruthlessness, indiscretion, and an urge toward control over the outside world. After Rousseau Judge has visited J.J., he agrees with J.J. that writers are arrogant, haughty, calculating, self-serving, proud, and distrustful, to list only a few of the terms applicable to the dark side of introversion, and indiscreet, controlling, and dependent on the outside world, to add a few of the extreme features of extraversion. In both the Judge's and J.J.'s opinion, this chain of defects can be traced back to a forgetting of one's initial reasons for turning to writing: to share one's ideas and soul with the other, rather than to learn to please and so control the other in order to satisfy one's own pride. The shift of focus from inner to outer world removes writing from its foundation in integrity and negates its wholeness by redefining it in terms of comparison with the other. With the extreme development and subsequent loss of basic introverted qualities, the normal process of compensation in the psychic system — enantiodromia — falters, and the misdirected energies of the paranoid, hypercritical side of creativity translate into extraverted behavior, paradoxically gaining control of the inner side. In the case at hand, this transformation may appear as a takeover by an ego wishing for gratification at the expense of the more objective and detached energies of the self. Having identified the writer of his time as a socializer rather than as a free spirit, Rousseau Judge sees the socialized writer (conversely to J.J.) as someone who favors his own personal interest and who does not hesitate to define himself by the control he wields over the external world, i.e., his audience.

J.J. is a recluse who cannot hate anybody because he lives alone and presents nothing of the writer in his temperament (Rousseau 1990, 116–117; 1959, 810–811). He is an outsider among writers who remains lucid about his status and does not hesitate to denounce the defects of the profession — and it is these defects that seem to be his unforgivable sins, as J.J. himself informs the Judge. The Judge sums up J.J.'s predicament thus: "For myself, I can imagine only this means to explain the different degrees of hatred people feel toward him, in proportion to how much those who indulge in it see themselves as deserving the reproaches he states about his century and his contemporaries" (1990, 177; 1959, 889).

Charlatanism and *amour-propre* are fundamental defects that trigger a multitude of other unforgivable traits, such as tyranny and intolerance. The charges J.J. makes against the *livriers* — book factories, as he calls them (1990, 139–141; 1959, 840–842) — explain their relentless plotting against him, since only he has had the courage to denounce the profession as well as the corruption of *l'esprit philosophe.* The League reflects a condition in which positive qualities of introverted thinking have transformed into negative extraverted qualities. These alterations reflect a failure to adhere to the purpose of writing — self-expression, not pleasing and controlling others. As a rebel within the profession, J.J. represents the conscience that the dark side of the profession has dismissed in adopting extraverted behaviors, themselves the result of introversion carried to extremes. Close analysis of J.J.'s character reveals how much Rousseau Judge, and through him J.J., have tried to dissociate J.J. the author from the world he denounces and that has retaliated against him (1990, 46–47; 1959, 810). The character of J.J., as described from both sides, appears terribly complex, yet he appears to embody all the positive qualities of the extraverted feeler. Or does he?

Having brought forth the complexities involved in sorting out the unconscious contents that led to neurosis and that threw the author Rousseau into a crisis of individuation, we can now analyze J.J.'s character in light of the oppositions of extraverted feeler and introverted thinker and see to what extent their integration constitutes a dilemma. Though for convenience's sake we have isolated "characters" in the *Dialogues* and identified them according to the fiction that the author Rousseau presents to us, we must not forget that in this work each constructed "character" reflects a fragment of Rousseau's own individual integrating process. If the Judge is the balanced introverted thinking type, the Frenchman an unintegrated extraverted feeling type, the writers and the League both introverted thinking and extraverted feeling types, though in degenerate states (i.e., in the shadow), then J.J., if we read his description rightly, represents the perfect embodiment of the positive extraverted feeling type. The Judge presents J.J. as natural, passionate, sensitive, and spontaneous, absolutely incapable of conniving, thinking for the sake of thinking — in brief, clumsy but loving, tactless yet human, a good extraverted feeler (Rousseau 1990, 113–118; 1959, 804–813). But looking more closely at the description of the Cyclops, the monster that J.J. says his enemies have made up, we see those qualities in J.J. that belong to his shadow — the very side he must integrate to achieve detachment.[10] The transformation from positive introversion to negative extraverted qualities attributed to the League reflects Rousseau the author's, or at least J.J.'s, transformation from a simple "natural" man to a successful author trapped in *amour-propre.* While he is explaining the contradictions in J.J., the Judge admits that his observations have led him to believe that J.J.'s temperament makes his behavior seem full of contradictions: "These observations and the others that relate to it [i.e., Rousseau Judge's knowledge of J.J.] offer as their outcome a mixed temperament composed of elements that appear contradictory" (1990, 111; 1959, 804).

We can distinguish two ways of tackling the aspect of contradiction in J.J. There are a priori contradictions that make J.J. the complex character he is and contradictions that J.J.'s enemies choose to single out. These latter contradictions might, in fact, be the ones that triggered the real Rousseau's crisis. The Judge's report to the Frenchman underlines the oppositions already presented from J.J.'s point of view. Like a mirror image, the grievances of the League toward J.J. seem mainly to concern *amour-propre.* Though J.J.'s *amour-propre* is not seen directly as a result of his profession, but rather as a result of his shyness, his pride and self-consciousness do seem crucial in the debate. Comparing the Judge's description of J.J. to the League's description of him, we find a series of blatant contradictions. In fact, the Judge suggests to the Frenchman that to know J.J., he must systematically attribute to him characteristics opposite those given to him by adversaries:

> For example, do you wish to have a concise idea of my observations? Take the exact opposite of everything, the good as well as the bad, of your gentlemen's J.J. and you will have very precisely the person I found. Theirs is cruel. ... Mine is gentle. ... Theirs is intractable. ... Mine is easygoing. ... Theirs [is] misanthropic. ... Mine, humane to excess [etc.].[11]

The oppositions are presented by the Judge in such a way that we would think of the League's judgments as sheer projection if we were not aware that this is Rousseau the author's fictitious account. Presented as a positive extraverted thinker, J.J. nevertheless manifests a Jungian shadow (the Cyclops) that J.J. attributes to his enemies. We can grant the author Rousseau a certain lucidity in recognizing this because he gives lucidity to the Judge in acknowledging that these opposing attributes may be misleading. At the end of his lengthy description, the Judge adds, "Isn't it true that if I were to multiply these oppositions, as I could do, you would take them for imaginary games that would have no reality?" (1990, 107; 1959, 798).

Looking at how the Judge defends J.J., it seems clear that J.J., like Rousseau the author, is a puzzle to himself. Obviously, Rousseau is trying to discover through the character of J.J. who he thinks he is, having after all chosen a career that seems in his eyes inappropriate to his temperament and convictions. Rousseau, alias J.J., is the sensual man of nature, not the reflecting man bound to other's opinions. If a sensual natural temperament will enable Rousseau to integrate in J.J. his contradictory extraverted and introverted qualities, it is quite significant that no real resolution occurs at the end of the third *Dialogue*. Only in the "History of the Preceding Writing" at the end of the book, where Rousseau describes his fevered anxiety regarding the delivery and reception of his manuscript, does he come to a resolution. Here, Rousseau describes how his initial efforts to "deliver" the manuscript relied on "Providence" (which we may interpret as actions dependent on resolution via outside or unconscious forces rather than through conscious will), behaving as "all unfortunates do who believe they see an explicit directive of fate in everything that happens to them" (1990, 250; 1959, 983). He inscribes the title page of a copy of the manuscript with the following message:

> Whoever you are whom Heaven has made the arbiter of this writing, whatever use you have resolved to make of it, and whatever opinion you have of the Author, this unfortunate Author implores you by your human pity and by the agonies he suffered in writing it, not to dispose of it until you have read the entire thing. (1990, 247–248; 1959, 979)

Rousseau attempts to leave this copy of the manuscript in Notre Dame Cathedral, believing it will somehow reach the king, but finding the entry to the church choir locked, decides that heaven itself has joined the conspiracy against him. "Providence" then sends him English visitors whom he feels he can trust, but one of them reads and comments on the manuscript as if it were a literary work, and to the other he gives only a partially completed draft. Frustrated, Rousseau makes several copies of a letter, "To all Frenchmen who still love justice and truth," and tries to "distribute them in parks and on the streets to those strangers whose faces most appealed to [him]" (1990, 251; 1959, 984). When his attempts meet with failure, a paroxysm of despair suddenly reverses the pole and makes him realize the pointlessness of his efforts, perhaps snapping him out of the state of projection that had led him to write the *Dialogues:* "[a] passage of *Emile* that I recalled made me return within myself and find what I had vainly sought outside" (1990, 252; 1959, 985).

The person individuating commonly can contemplate the symbol of transformation only after the hidden, unconscious content has been let out. The mandala and the steps involved in its creation thus are apropos. By giving up all desire to justify himself in the eyes of the public, Rousseau overcomes *amour-propre,* an obvious part of his shadow. Rousseau's peace of mind after his creation and failed attempts at dissemination of the *Dialogues* is a direct result of an inwardly accomplished gesture. The *Dialogues* does not acknowledge this situation directly or rationally, but we can see that Rousseau intuitively solves his problem. Through the creation of the mandala that underlies the structure of the *Dialogues,* Rousseau is able to attain peace with himself—an outcome that, in fact, becomes fully apparent only later in the *Reveries.*

Endnotes

1. Rousseau scholar, critic, and translator Allan Bloom states that amour-propre is "the central term in Rousseau's psychology. ... Ordinarily, in its non-'extended sense,' it would be translated as vanity or pride, but it is a word too full of nuance and too important ... not to be ... revealed in its full subtlety. It is usually opposed to amour de soi. Both expressions mean self-love. Rousseau, instead of opposing love of self to love of others, opposes two kinds of self-love, a good and bad form. Thus without abandoning the view of modern political philosophy that man is primarily concerned with himself—particularly his own preservation—he is able to avoid Hobbes' conclusion that men, as a result of their selfishness, are necessarily in competition with one another. His earliest statement on this issue—the foundation of his argument that man is naturally good—is Discourse on the Origins of Inequality, note XV: 'Amour-propre and amour de soi, two passions very different in their nature and in their effects, must not be confused. Love of oneself is a natural sentiment which inclines every animal to watch over its own preservation, and which directed in man by reason and modified by pity, produces humanity and virtue. Amour-propre is only a relative sentiment, artificial, and born in society, which inclines each individual to have a greater esteem for himself than for anyone else, inspires in all the harm they do to one another, and is the true source of honor'" (Bloom 1979, 483–484).

2. The English version will be cited as Rousseau 1990, and the French quotations in the notes will be cited as Rousseau 1959. I have made a few changes in the English passages, often reflecting clarifications suggested by Dr. Dennis Turner, the editor of this article, whose thoroughness, dedication, and helpful suggestions have been invaluable to the completion of this project. I take full responsibility for all alterations to the translations. All changes to Bush, Kelly, and Masters are noted in the citations. In the French citations the spellings reflect Rousseau's idiosyncratic usage as presented in the definitive NRF/Gallimard Pléiade edition of this and other works by Rousseau.

3. The interpretation of the stages of individuation offered here is largely inspired by a series of seminars presented by M. Stein in 1989 (1991). This discussion emphasizes stages of growth in individual consciousness rather than stages of socialization or other interpretations of individuation. The description of individuation Stein gives in these seminars is further amplified in his discussion "The Five Stages of Consciousness," in Jung's Map of the Soul (1998, 179–189). It should be noted that other depth psychologists may recognize different processes and numbers of steps underlying the individuation process.

   According to Stein's interpretation, individuation unifies the conscious and unconscious systems of psychic matter. This unification occurs thanks to the spontaneous generation of one or more symbols contributing to the psychic blossoming of the individual. Jung distinguishes two fundamental phases in this psychic growth, which in turn can be divided into five consecutive stages in the development of consciousness. The two phases are first the unification of the ego complex and second individuation itself—that is to say, the return to the mother in which the ego complex seeks to unite with the unconscious and with the archetype of the self. This last stage usually occurs in the second half of life.

   Since consciousness only develops over time, it is possible to identify several degrees of growth in its formation. Jung calls the first level of growth the state of "participation mystique," a term borrowed from the ethnologist Levy-Bruhl. At this level, the individual identifies himself fully with the surrounding world. Not aware of this state, he or she lives in complete projection onto the world as a unity. No separation between self and other occurs; all is mysteriously linked.

The second stage of growth involves localized projections. The self begins to distinguish self from other and establishes boundaries between subject and object. At this point, the individual tends to limit projection to certain persons in whom he or she invests omnipotent and omniscient qualities. The third stage of growth involves a transition from concrete to abstract projections, leading the individual to recognize the world as an objective terrain wherein he or she no longer permanently confronts the object. Projection takes place at the level of vision or ideology, but nonetheless remains projection. Only at the fourth stage does the phenomenon of projection seem to undergo what Stein calls a "radical extinction" (1998, 183) during a process of ego inflation; the individual no longer projects onto God, the world, or some ideology. Everything becomes contingent at this point; and through a relativizing of values, the ego, swollen with its own importance, risks falling into disillusion, delusion, paranoia, or megalomania. The fifth level establishes a state of recognition in which conscious and unconscious systems unite, allowing delineation of the point where ego ends and the contents of the unconscious begin. This return, which involves internal communication, is directly linked to the transcendent functioning of unifying symbols that map out the individual's psychic reality. The phenomenon of individuation generally involves recognizing these boundaries and internalizing psychic matter and mental contents.

4. In 1745, Rousseau became involved with Thérèse Levasseur, a servant with no education with whom he lived, though the two were married only much later in life. Presumably he had several children with her, all of whom were placed in orphanages. The nature of Rousseau's relationship with Thérèse, as well as the paternity of her children, is debated.

5. "The League" refers to the masterminds of the plot against Rousseau. For our purposes, it is mostly a psychological projection with a basis in objective reality. "The League," also referred to as "the Gentlemen" and "the Authors of the plot" or just "the Authors," had at its core Diderot, Grimm, and Mme. d'Epinay, and as its co-conspirators d'Alembert, Tronchin, and other persons spreading in a nefarious mesh to include (in Rousseau's mind and perhaps in reality) the governments and citizenry of France, Geneva, Bern, and so on. Rousseau saw the work of the League, with some justification, as being behind the efforts to arrest him in France, his expulsion from Bern, and other incidents of real and imagined persecution.

6. "An active heart and a lazy nature must inspire the taste for reverie. This taste emerges and becomes a very lively passion if it is helped in the slightest by the imagination. This is what very often happens to Orientals. It is what happened to J.J" (Rousseau 1990, 120); «Un cœur actif et un naturel paresseux doivent inspirer le gout de la rêverie. Ce gout perce et devient une passion très vive, pour peu qu'il soit secondé par l'imagination. C'est ce qui arrive très frequemment aux Orientaux; c'est ce qui est arrivé à J.J.» (Rousseau 1959, 816).

7. I have altered the translation slightly. The translation by Bush, Kelly, and Masters reads, "He attained and passed maturity without thinking of writing books, and without feeling for a moment the need for that fatal celebrity. ... It was even, in a way, by surprise and without forming the project that he found himself thrust into that fatal career. ... " (1990, 130–131); «Il atteignit et passa l'age mûr sans songer à faire des livres, et sans sentir un instant le besoin de cette célébrité fatale. ... Ce fut même en quelque façon par surprise et sans en avoir formé le projet qu'il se trouva jetté dans cette funeste carriére. ... Une malheureuse question d'Academie qu'il lut dans un Mercure vint tout à coup ... lui montrer un autre univers, un véritable âge d'or ..., et réaliser en espérance toutes ses visions. ... De la vive effervescence qui se fit alors dans son ame sortirent ces etincelles de génie qu'on a vu briller dans ses écrits durant dix ans de délire et de fiévre ...» (1959, 827–829).

8. "Through dreams one becomes acquainted with aspects of one's own personality that for various reasons one has preferred not to look at too closely. This is what Jung called 'the realization of the shadow.' (He used the term 'shadow' for this unconscious part of the personality because it actually often appears in dreams in a personified form.) The shadow is not the whole of the unconscious personality. It represents unknown or little-known attributes and qualities of the ego — aspects that mostly belong to the personal sphere and that could just as well be conscious. ... When an individual makes an attempt to see his shadow, he becomes aware of (and often ashamed of) those qualities and impulses he denies in himself but can plainly see in other people — such things as egotism, mental laziness, and sloppiness. ..." (Jung 1964, 168).

9. I have altered the translation. The translation by Bush, Kelly, and Masters reads, "Your promise, which you cannot break without violating your faith, has no other limits than life ... "(1990, 32); «Votre engagement, auquel vous ne pouvez manquer sans violer votre foi, n'a quant à sa durée d'autres bornes que celles de la vie ... . [V]ous devez concourir avec tout le monde à lui faire ignorer toujours ce qu'on sait et comment on le sait» (1959, 699–700).

10. See Rousseau Judge's comment to the Frenchman: "I don't mean to give you as realities all the troubling ideas suggested to J.J. by the profound obscurities in which they [i.e., the League] persist in surrounding him. The mysteries made for him about everything are so black it is not surprising

that they affect his frightened imagination with the same coloration" (1990, 92). «Je ne prétends pas vous donner pour des réalités toutes les idées inquietantes que fournit à J.J. l'obscurité profonde dont on s'applique à l'entourer. Les mistéres qu'on lui fait de tout ont un aspect si noir qu'il n'est pas surprenant qu'ils affectent de la même teinte son imagination effarouchée» (1959, 780).

11. I have altered the translation. The translation by Bush, Kelly, and Masters reads, "Theirs [is] a ferocious misanthrope...." (1990, 106); «Voulez-vous, par exemple, avoir un sommaire de mes observations? Prenez directement et en tout, tant en bien qu'en mal le contrepied du J. J. de vos Messieurs, vous aurez très exactement celui que j'ai trouvé. Le leur est cruel.... Le mien est doux.... Le leur est intraitable.... Le mien est facile.... Le leur est misanthrope.... Le mien humain jusqu'à l'excès [etc.]...» (1959, 797–798).

BIBLIOGRAPHY

Bloom, Allan, trans. 1979. *Emile by Jean-Jacques Rousseau.* [n.p.]: Basic Books.

Cranston, Maurice 1982. *Jean-Jacques: The Early Life and Work of Jean-Jacques Rousseau, 1712-1754.* New York: Norton, 1982.

——. 1991. *The Noble Savage: Jean-Jacques Rousseau, 1754-1762.* Chicago: University of Chicago Press.

——. 1997. *The Solitary Self: Jean-Jacques Rousseau in Exile and Adversity.* Chicago: University of Chicago Press.

Jung, C.G. 1964. "Approaching the Unconscious." In *Man and His Symbols,* eds. C.G. Jung and M.-L. Von Franz., 18–103. New York: Anchor, 1964.

——. 1968. "Psychology and Alchemy," CW 12, ¶96

——. 1971. "Psychological Types," CW 6, ¶¶419–420.

Meier, C.A. 1989. *Consciousness.* Trans. David N. Roscoe. Boston: Sigo.

Rousseau, Jean-Jacques. 1990. *Rousseau Judge of Jean-Jacques: Dialogues. Collected Writings of Rousseau 1.* Trans. Judith R. Bush, Christopher Kelly, and Roger D. Masters. Eds. Roger D. Masters and Christopher Kelly. Hanover, NH: Dartmouth College/UP New England. Translated from *Rousseau juge de Jean Jaques: Dialogues.* Ed. Robert Osmont. *Les Confessions. Autres textes autobiographiques.* Eds. Bernard Gagnebin and Marcel Raymond. *Œuvres complètes de Rousseau I.* 657–992. (Paris: NRF/Gallimard, 1959).

——. 1995. "The Confessions." *The Confessions and Correspondence, Including the Letters to Malesherbes. Collected Writings of Rousseau 5.* Trans. Christopher Kelly. Ed. Christopher Kelly, Roger D. Masters, and Peter J. Stillman. Hanover, NH: Dartmouth College/UP New England. Translated from *Les Confessions. Autres textes autobiographiques.* Ed. Bernard Gagnebin and Marcel Raymond. *Œuvres complètes de Rousseau I.* 1–656. (Paris: NRF/Gallimard, 1959).

Spoto, Angelo. 1995. *Jung's Typology in Perspective.* Rev. ed. Wilmette, IL: Chiron.

Starobinski, Jean. 1971. *Jean-Jacques Rousseau: La transparence et l'obstacle.* Paris: Gallimard.

Stein, Murray. 1991. *The Jungian Psyche.* C.G. Jung Institute. Evanston, Illinois: Audiotape Series 458.

——. 1998. *Jung's Map of the Soul.* Chicago: Open Court, 1998.

Villaverde, Maria Jose. 1995. "Rousseau-Diderot: L'antagonisme de deux visions du monde." *Rousseau and Criticism / Rousseau et la critique,* Eds. Lorraine Clark and Guy Lafrance. Pensée libre 5: 33–47.

Von Franz, M.-L. 1964. "The Process of Individuation." *Man and His Symbols.* Eds. Carl G. Jung and M.-L. Von Franz. 158–229. New York: Anchor.

ABSTRACT

GUILLEMETTE JOHNSTON, "Archetypal Patterns of Behavior: A Jungian Analysis of the Mandala Structure in the *Dialogues* of Jean-Jacques Rousseau." JUNG JOURNAL: CULTURE & PSYCHE, 1:4, 43-68. This study argues that Jean-Jacques Rousseau's autobiographical work, *Rousseau Judge of Jean-Jacques: Dialogues,* provides a reflection of the process of individuation as described in analytical psychology. Rousseau's *Dialogues,* a series of fictional conversations inspired by actual occurrences, is viewed in relation to the structural pattern of the mandala, a pattern that Jung saw as offering an archetypal representation of balance in reaction to disturbances of psychic equilibrium. The crisis Rousseau faced while writing the *Dialogues* involved the merging of introverted thinking with extraverted feeling, bringing conscious ego together with unconscious content. Rousseau articulated this merging through spontaneously creating a literary mandala that joins fiction and reality via three dialogues in which opposing voices interact and gradually move toward reconciliation. Because the *Dialogues* is only one of Rousseau's autobiographical texts, this study positions the *Dialogues* in Rousseau's œuvres and gives insight into his understanding of his intentions in writing the *Dialogues* and other works. It presents a brief biography of Rousseau and also offers background to and a summary of the *Dialogues.* Finally, it analyzes the *Dialogues* in light of Jung's quaternary analysis of the psyche.

KEY WORDS

Jean-Jacques Rousseau, *Rousseau Judge of Jean-Jacques: Dialogues,* mandala, individuation, autobiography, Jung, depth psychology, psychological types

TELL ME ANOTHER MORNING

AN AUTOBIOGRAPHICAL NOVEL Zdena Berger

(Zdena Price, by permission)

JUNG JOURNAL: CULTURE & PSYCHE, FALL 2007, VOL. 1, NO. 4, 70-90

BOOK REVIEWS

A Survivor's Tale

Review of Zdena Berger's *Tell Me Another Morning.*
Ashfield, Massachusetts: Paris Press, 2007

THOMAS B. KIRSCH

This extraordinary book tells the tale of a 14-year-old girl named Tania who is living in Prague when she and her family are taken from their home by the Nazis. The book describes what happens to Tania and her family. With the help of two other girls, they all survive the concentration and labor camps, and they remain in contact after the war. This précis gives just the bare outline of what this book is about, however. Words cannot describe the experience of reading this autobiographical novel. It is so poetic and lyrical and the experiences so simply stated that it is like no other book on the Holocaust experience I have ever read.

Now it is being republished by Paris Press with a beautiful cover by Charlotte Salomon, also a victim of the Holocaust but who did not survive. The book also includes a lovely new afterward by the author. It is an extraordinary book.

What makes the writing so meaningful is that the experiences "Tania" goes through are simply stated without any exaggeration or unnecessary drama. The experiences are simply there. The Nazis are never mentioned as such, but are seen as those men in the "green uniforms." At times, one almost forgets this story is taking place in a concentration camp, but then one is suddenly jolted back to the tremendous hardships that they all had to endure. The spirits of the three girls flag at times, but they support each other through those difficulties.

It is hard to single out a particular anecdote in the book as being the most moving. The entire concentration camp experience is simply so other-worldly and the return to "normal" life requires such an adjustment that the author's graceful telling of the story is simply amazing.

The book is short. Indeed, the chapters read like parts of a poem. Because of the subject matter, it is a difficult book to read; however, the fact that "Tania" and her friends survive is a tribute to the human spirit.

THOMAS B. KIRSCH, M.D., is a psychiatrist in private practice in Palo Alto, California. He has served as president of the C.G. Jung Institute of San Francisco and of the International Association for Analytical Psychology (IAAP). He has written numerous articles and reviews and speaks frequently on clinical and historical topics. His book, *The Jungians*, has recently been translated into German, and he is the co-editor of *Initiation: The Living Reality of an Archetype*, published in 2007 by Routledge. *Correspondence*: 945 Middlefield Rd, Palo Alto, CA 94301, USA

ABSTRACT

THOMAS B. KIRSCH, "A Survivor's Tale," Review of Zdena Berger's *Tell Me Another Morning*, Paris Press, 2007, JUNG JOURNAL: CULTURE & PSYCHE, 1:4, 70-72. This is an autobiographical novel of a teenage Czechoslovakian Jewish girl who is torn away from her family during World War II. She is sent to several of the concentration camps and survives the camps and the war.

The author describes her arduous experience with great simplicity, and how with the aid of two other girls, they are all able to survive the most difficult hardships. The author then moves to California in 1955 to begin a new life.

KEY WORDS

Zdena Berger Price, Holocaust, Terezin, Bergen-Belsen, labor camps, Prague, Czechoslovakia, survival, Charlotte Salomon, Jews

The Subtle Power of Silence

Review of Robert Sardello's *Silence*.
Benson, North Carolina: Goldenstone Press, 2006.

DENNIS PATRICK SLATTERY

I prefer to be up most mornings by 4 a.m. In these quiet hours before darkness reluctantly gives way to the light in our canyon north of Santa Barbara, I read, meditate, write, and truth be told, enjoy the darkness and the Silence. When I miss a morning's early hours of Silence, the day that follows seems off-center, a bit eccentric, and unbalanced. Such is Silence's power to establish one's own inner gravity at the beginning of a day.

Robert Sardello's new book on Silence confirms many of the verities I have sensed about the power of this essential quality of life. His earlier books, *Facing the World with Soul, Freeing the Soul from Fear,* and *Love and the Soul,* to name a few, testify to a characteristic that I have always admired in his work and in his person: he is a bit of a mystic. I say this less to praise him than to place him, to afford him a context within Silence. Each chapter begins with what I wish to call a "lyric interlude," in which his wife, Cheryl Sanders-Sardello offers a one-page poetic reflection on the theme of the chapter to follow. Her penetrating reveries push back the cuticle of Silence

DENNIS PATRICK SLATTERY, Ph.D., is Core Faculty, Mythological Studies at Pacifica Graduate Institute in Carpinteria, California. He is the author or co-editor of eleven books and dozens of book reviews and articles in journals, magazines, and newspapers. A few of his titles include *The Wounded Body: Remembering the Markings of Flesh;* with Lionel Corbett, *Depth Psychology: Meditations in the Field;* and *Psychology at the Threshold.* His current publications include *Harvesting Darkness: Essays on Literature, Myth, Film and Culture* as well as *A Limbo of Shards: Essays on Memory, Myth and Metaphor.* He has published two volumes of poetry with accompanying CDs, *Casting the Shadows: Selected Poems* and *Just Below the Water Line: Selected Poems,* and has just completed a third volume of poetry, *Twisted Sky: Selected Poems,* to be published in 2007. *Correspondence:* 4690 River Oaks Drive, New Braunfels, TX, 78132, USA to expose its further power. Thus, this is a co-created work that breaks new ground in our understanding of Silence as a way of knowing as well as a way of being.

As a phenomenological psychologist, a therapist, a writer fully conversant with the works of Jung, Freud, Gaston Bachelard, Rudolph Steiner, Henry Corbin, and the mystical tradition, as well as co-founder of the School of Spiritual Psychology in North Carolina, Sardello has developed a unique voice in what might be called a psychology of reverie, or an imaginal psychology of spirit. Although his writing is meditative, it carries a cutting-edge precision that invites reverie and dream rather than heady analysis; it promotes a poetics of soul over a partitioning of the person. As a cultural psychologist, he peels back the skin of a fear-based, consumer-driven mythos to reveal the hidden power in Silence, meditation, and prayer as antibodies to such debilitating conditions.

Sardello's meditation on Silence follows in the tradition of one of the most poignant portraits I have ever encountered, Max Picard's *The World of Silence*. There Picard claims that "to take language from silence we have made language an orphan. The tongue we speak today is no longer a mother-tongue but an orphaned tongue" (1988, 41). Sardello's own study retrieves the orphan from a culture that not only denies Silence but also actively suppresses it. Silence is not good for business, and the business at hand is to consume, to remain distracted, to fill our lives with the noisiness that Silence denies and, in so doing, to remain oblivious.

Sardello's ideas on Silence are both bold and big: "Our body's center is the necessary meeting point of where the inward silence of solitude meets up with the great Silence of Cosmic Wisdom" (2006, 8). In his scope and range of connection between Silence and the created order, Sardello thinks epically of Silence's orbit, not unlike the grand scheme of mythologist Joseph Campbell as he addresses the circumference of myth. My own sense is that Silence is as big as myth both in the individual soul and in the larger atmosphere of the cosmos.

A powerful and penetrating Introduction by Therese Schroeder-Sheker outlines Sardello's inspired prose best: "I had begun to wonder if the author hadn't had an unspoken Moses-by-the-Burning-Bush experience, and if, in the limitless Love of that non-consuming fire, this burning, radiant, urgent Silence emerged for him as a hidden name for Christ" (Sardello 2006, xvii–xix). Perhaps *glow* over *burning* might also capture Sardello's mystical musing on Silence's power. For like Max Picard's, another voice that echoes in Sardello's exploration of Silence's many voices, is the poet John Keats, who immortalized Silence's power in one of his most famous poems, "Ode on a Grecian Urn":

Thou still unravish'd bride
  of quietness,
Thou foster-child of silence
  and slow time,
Sylvan historian, who canst
  thus express
A flowery tale more sweetly
  than our rhyme:
(1959, 207, Stanza 1)

Keats and Sardello share a common affinity for Silence's power to speak, as it were, more poignantly than words themselves often have the capacity to enjoin.

Perusing the Table of Contents reveals the facets of Silence as an elaborate mosaic of knowing. To name a few chapter titles: "A Meditation on Silence," "The Guardian of Silence," "Entering the Silence," "Making a Clearing for Silence," and "Silence,

Prayer, and Meditation." That the word is capitalized throughout his study, which I follow here, makes Silence a proper, not a common, noun. Such a designation is apt, because the way Sardello works Silence's equi-vocal nature places it, for me, in the domain of an archetype, perhaps what C.G. Jung himself called "an archetype of transformation." Jung develops what he means: "They are not personalities, but are typical situations, places, ways and means, that symbolize the kind of transformation in question" (CW 9/1, ¶80). Perhaps it is more accurate to say that Silence is more akin to an energy field than simply the absence of sound or noise. This latter idea is far too narrow, though, and actually a provincial attitude toward Silence, as Sardello explores the complex strata of Silence's geography.

For him, Silence is engaged. He lists several of its features: it is not spatial; it whirls, so it is not linear; it is subtle and complexly layered and contains many degrees of depth (Sardello 2006, 37–38). According to Sardello, Silence is not a passive state but a condition of receptivity with mysterious qualities. It provides the one in Silence a "meditative attention" that opens one to the other — contrary to the brand of egoistic Silence that wounds another person by withholding self from her or him, which is a form of power over another (41). Silence that promotes meditation, by contrast, is an imaginal act of openness.

An area I found particularly provocative is one in which the author develops the place and presence of Silence in conversation with others. Silence, he observes, actually creates "a holy third" in conversation if we imagine a conversation with another that consists of two overlapping circles; the place of the overlap is the vesica; it is, for Sardello, "the space of the holy third" (2006, 44). In a sense that Jung would appreciate, Sardello reveals that when two people are relating, a "third presence is entailed." Such an interactive field created between the one and the two to create a third, he suggests, "is more ineffable than any archetypal god or goddess" (45). Rather, as psychology's impulse moves its theory to reveal how "relating" is in the service of having a better relationship, Sardello turns this notion by suggesting that one intrinsic value to relationships is that they can lead the two people into Silence; Silence's nature is to be relational (48).

As Sardello develops the theory and imagination of Silence and, in the process, offers various exercises to promote a depth of Silence in the reader, Sanders-Sardello offers more intimate lyric interludes on Silence:

Entering your room I know I am not alone with you. A holy silence attends you, too, close to your head just there by the window. It seems to have a proprietary attitude, as if you belong more to silence than to me. (2006, 50)

As Silence itself is layered, it seems that the two authors wish to claim such layering in the structure and in the perspectives each takes up toward this mysterious human quality of being. Both, in addition, move their meditations on Silence to the world of healing and Spiritual presenting, where Silence enwombs the one engaging its encompassing orbit. Sardello, in particular, again writes against the grain of conventional, clichéd thought on spiritual realities, which tend to be placed "out there" somewhere. His intention is to realign thought to allow not "thinking about, but thinking within" spiritual realities (69).

In making such a move, the author aligns himself with another mystic poet, this time of the fourteenth century, Dante Alighieri. Here is how. As Dante's *Commedia* is a poetic meditation on the way Love itself is a form of intelligence, what he termed *"intelleto de amore,"* so does Sardello want to entertain how Silence is a "mode of Intelligence, a form of Intelligence." In fact, it is a form of Wisdom: "As we enter into Silence, we enter into Wisdom" (2006, 69). For Sardello, such a move of the imagination allows us to be present to the world in what seems a vulnerable, open, and porous posture. It also seems to include being present in an engaged and unique way. But forces in the culture mitigate against such a posture.

He calls those energies that work against Silence, spirit, and a vulnerable presence to things "death forces" that are found in everything prepackaged and that require "from us only to consume" (Sardello 2006, 71). A deadness of soul is the consequence of such thoughtless consumption. Returning to his earlier study, *Freeing the Soul from Fear,* he believes that one of today's prepackages on sale for mass consumption is fear. Silence counteracts such a movement in the soul by promoting and engaging what Sardello calls clearing: "There are connections between inner clearing and the practices of religious traditions, particularly to the mystical tradition and initiatory practices...." (74). Two qualities would appear to accompany this clearing: assent and grace. Whereas "assent is a creative act [that] opens the inner heart space for something to be created rather than just performed," grace is a greater mystery: "Grace is the permeation of our soul with divine love. It is a very palpable bodily feeling. It feels as if we are accompanied by a radiance,..." (77). What his study on Silence seems to be leading us to is a softening of a sclerosis of the heart (a hardening of the heart's arteries) so that we yield into our lives and into of the lives of others in a more creative and uniquely personal way. It is also the way

into an authentic imaginal life, one that is poetic rather than pedestrian, relational rather than solitary, contemplative rather than consuming.

At the close of his original and engaging exploration, Sardello adumbrates three aspects of the heart's spirituality worth listing here: "The heart lives in service. The heart lives in healing. The heart lives in worship....They are the primary currents of Silence that together constitute reverence" (2006, 88). His thoughts on these three attributes or currents of Silence are remarkably close to the Dalai Lama's philosophy of Buddhism outlined in his *Guide to the Bodhisattva's Way of Life* (1994). Both writers engage practices whose intention is to dissolve the furious autonomy of the individual, a condition the Dalai Lama would call a grand illusion, in order to serve others out of compassion.

For Sardello, prayer, service, and joy comprise what he calls "the spiritual alchemy of the heart," which liberates the one to invest in the other within a radiance of divine love (2006, 88). Silence is a mystical and mysterious third entity that we might cultivate to deepen our presence and to promote images of unselfishness for others as example. My own sense is that Silence, this one word with multiple experiences appended to it, could be the seed of an entire therapy — a therapy "of silence and slow time" (1959, 207).

BIBLIOGRAPHY

Dalai Lama. 1994. *A Flash of Lightning in the Dark of Night: A Guide to the Bodhisattva's Way of Life.* Trans. The Padmakara Translation Group. New York: Shambhala Dragon Editions.

Jung, C.G. 1954. "Archetypes of the Collective Unconscious," *Collected Works* 9/1, ¶80, Princeton, NJ: Princeton University Press.

Keats, John. 1959. *Selected Poems and Letters by John Keats.* Ed. Douglas Bush.
New York: Riverside Editions.

Picard, Max. 1988. *The World of Silence.*
Washington, DC: Gateway.

Sardello, Robert. 2006. *Silence.* Benson,
NC: Goldenstone Press.

ABSTRACT

DENNIS PATRICK SLATTERY, "The Subtle Power of Silence," Review of Robert
Sardello's *Silence.* Benson, North Carolina:
Goldenstone Press, 2006, JUNG JOURNAL:
CULTURE & PSYCHE, 1:4, 72-76. Traditionally,
silence has been understood as the absence
of noise or equated with quiet. Robert
Sardello, therapist, spiritual director, and
poet of the soul, sees such designations
as actually suffocating silence. His study,
with co-author Cheryl Sanders-Sardello,
reimagines Silence from the perspectives of
depth psychology, religious spiritual traditions, therapy, as well as phenomenology.
His work uncovers the complex, repetitive,
spiralic, and healing powers of silence, its
essential place as a third element in human
relations and a productive force that opens
one to the potentially creative aspect of one's
own being. Death forces, by contrast, in the
form of consumer culture, prepackage life
and experience to be consumed, not lived
creatively. Sardello's book has far-reaching
implications for therapy, education, and
politics to name a few.

KEY WORDS

silence, joy, love, spiritual, consumer culture, death forces, alchemy of the heart,
wisdom, healing.

Seeing in the Dark Light of the Soul

Review of Ronald Schenk's *Dark Light:*
The Appearance of Death in Everyday Life.
Albany: State University of New York Press, 2001.

ROBERT ROMANYSHYN

When I was asked to review Dark Light: The Appearance of Death
in Everyday Life, *written by the Jungian analyst Ronald Schenk, I accepted
immediately for two reasons. First, I accepted because I have always been
intrigued by the author's style. He has a graceful and fluid pen, and as a reader
of some of his earlier essays and books, I have always come away not only with
an appreciation for his keen insights, but also with a sense of delight for the ways
in which my ear has been so charmingly seduced into the pleasures of his words.
Who would not be charmed, for example, by the following passage from the
section entitled, "Nosing The Face: An Introduction":*

ROBERT ROMANYSHYN, Ph.D., is a core faculty member of Pacifica Graduate Institute
and the author of *Ways of the Heart, Mirror and Metaphor, Soul in Grief,* and *Technology
as Symptom and Dream. Correspondence:* Pacifica Graduate Institute, 249 Lambert Road,
Carpinteria, CA, 93013, USA. E-mail: romany@pacifica.edu.

In preparing this book for publication, I was reminded of my family's history of attempts at production and salesmanship. My great-grandfather made glue in factories at different locations across the Midwest. His problem was that he could not get any of the factories to stick together. They would fall apart financially, and he would have to move on to another town and start all over again. His son, my grandfather, traveled to schools in the city of Chicago to sell maps. Inevitably, he would get lost on the way and had to bring my grandmother along to navigate. Now, while I am writing a book that has to do with beauty and vision, I can hear a voice in the background saying, "But Ron, what about your appearance?!" (Schenk 2001, 1)

From the opening paragraph the reader is hooked and wants to nose around with this guy for a spell because there is something of the trickster in him, something that delights the ear and touches the heart.

Second, I accepted the invitation to write this review because I was also intrigued by the title, *Dark Light*. What images are conjured up by that phrase, especially for a phenomenologist like myself with a long-standing interest in reverie as a mode of perceiving the world with my eyes "wide shut," as if in a dream while awake. Ronald Schenk's book takes us into the dreams of cultural events, and in their exploration, he awakens us to those half-illuminated places where the forgotten soul of the event lingers in the shadows. In this sense, *Dark Light* is as much about a way of seeing events as it is about the events to be seen. But the author does not tell us that until the penultimate sentence of the last essay prior to the Epilogue. In that sentence he writes,

"Dark light ultimately is both seen and a way of seeing, image and imagination" (Schenk 2001, 150). He does not tell us until the end, nor does he have to, because, like a good teacher, he shows us how to imagine the dreams of cultural events along the way. His small, elegant book is a kind of education into the imagination, practiced as he brings us along on his eight cultural journeys, an education into those moments of death in everyday life where we encounter a challenge to preformed and unexamined ways of thinking and being, where we encounter a death of the ego's familiar ways of being in the world. In dark light, he writes, death "...is a metaphor for imagination's undermining, both subtle and overt, of our heroic, ego-oriented attitude toward life" (3).

The eight essays that comprise the book deal with a range of cultural themes arranged into four parts. "Part One: Death as Beauty" is, for me, the place where the author is at his phenomenological best. Phenomenology is nothing if it is not first of all a celebration of appearances, of the splendor of the perceived world in all its wonder and mystery, and in this celebration, there is an element of healing as phenomenology restores us to the world, re-members the broken connection between body as living flesh and the skin of the world, and recovers the bond of Eros between the sensing, sensitive flesh and the sensuous world.

In the first chapter, "Beauty as Healer," Schenk draws upon his extensive experience working with the Navajo Indians, and through their ways of experiencing the world, we begin to remember what we have lost in erecting a barrier between subject and object. This chapter is, indeed, a work of anamnesis, of un-forgetting, a kind of homecoming, which is phenomenology. His reminiscences on language and perception in this chapter have a gem-like quality. They sparkle and have a bittersweet sense, which opens our hearts to those moments when we knew the world was alive. Reflecting on one of those moments, he says, "It was my experience that Navajo children begin having serious problems with the white educational system in the third grade, when they start learning the syntax of English grammar, which splits the subject and the object" (Schenk 2001, 11). When I read this passage, I recalled how the poet e. e. cummings once said

who pays any attention
to the syntax of things
will never wholly kiss you

(1954, 35, stanza 1)

Beauty as healer is a way of being kissed by the world, embraced by it, an intimacy of mutual seductions, examples of which thread themselves throughout this chapter. In the chapter "Beauty as Appearance," Schenk continues these explorations into beauty, and he sketches for us how beauty is a form of action and knowledge as well as the face of Being. In all these epiphanies of Beauty, the ego conscious mind is undone by the image and the ways in which beauty opens the imagination.

"Part Two: Death as Invisible" has two chapters, "Ball/Play: the Soul of the Game" and "Spirit in the Tube: The Life of Television." Beginning with his own dreams of becoming a ball player, Ron Schenk deepens the mystery of the game through an extended analysis of the Mayan myth of the Popol Vuh. A ballgame figures prominently in this myth, and through the myth, he shows us quite convincingly how playing the game connects us with the underworld and hence with death.

The reader cannot come away from this chapter without wondering about the national pastime of baseball and, indeed, Americans' obsession with all forms of sport. Has play as entertainment and business become too serious? Has it lost its ludic sense and its power to situate us in the liminal space between worlds? Perhaps, but these questions are not at the heart of the matter in this chapter. Rather, what informs this chapter is its power to awaken us to what we have forgotten, this connection between play, the gods, the underworld, and death. The ball in the game always has a will of its own and, in this respect, playing the game is entering the arena where we risk the will of our subjectivity. And so, while reading this chapter, I was reminded of a game I used to play when I was a child. Living on the fourth floor of an apartment building, I would bounce the ball against the steps above me as I climbed the four flights to where I lived. If the ball got past me, I would have to retrieve it and begin the ascent again. Moreover, the possibility always existed that in getting past me, the ball could fall into the cellar of the building, a dark place of haunting shadows to which I would have to descend to find it. It was a test of wills as it were, an early, unconscious confrontation with the underworld, an experiment with the "gods" of chance. How splendid it was for me to remember that moment and how extraordinary for a book that is so simple in its style and so wise in its simplicity to be able to do that!

"Spirit in the Tube: The Life of Television" takes up this cultural enterprise as a shared symptom. Recounting the criticisms made of television, of how, for example, it often functions like an addiction, Schenk nevertheless goes against the grain of these criticisms to retrieve what television as a cultural symptom might be asking us to remember. His reply is that the intention of the life of television "...is to unite spirit or invisible life with material or visible life to make psychological 'image'" (2001, 68). In this respect, he likens this intention to the work of alchemy, which also endeavored to unite spirit and matter. Like the alchemist would slip into reverie before his fire, within which he would behold his visions, the cool fire of television also induces a state of reverie, if not hypnosis, within which we behold its visions.

For the author, this technological magic, whose origins he rightly traces to the Renaissance development of linear perspective vision, "...becomes an attempt to transcend the tyranny of subjective 'I-ness' through contemplation, sleep and death" (Schenk 2001, 68). It is a bold thesis and one with which I agree because it attempts to unveil the god in the technology, which was the point of my own book *Technology As Symptom and Dream* (Romanyshyn 1989/2000). But I hesitate to endorse it fully because the collective consciousness that gathers around television in particular and technology in general seems more to be about the eclipse of the gods than about their recollection. Indeed, I wondered as I read this chapter if with television consciousness as exemplar of the age of technology, we have gone beyond the possibility of living a reflective psychological life. Schenk acknowledges this danger, but perhaps he is more hopeful. In any case, his reflections on the spirit in the tube are provocative, insightful, and worth our consideration.

In "Part Three: Death as Experience," Schenk explores the imagination of death in relationships. The chapter on fathers and sons is rich with insights from poetry, mythology, and religion, all of which show how "Separation and sacrifice are part of father/son togetherness" (Schenk 2001, 75). The range of his scholarship here is truly impressive as is the ease with which he commands his sources. Quoting a brief poem from Rumi, for example, Schenk manages to inscribe in the reader's mind this pregnant image of the relation between fathers and sons (73; Bly et al. 1992):

Your old grandmother says,
'Maybe you shouldn't go to school.
You look a little pale.'
Run when you hear that.
A father's stern slaps are better.
Your bodily soul wants comforting.
The severe father wants spiritual
*   clarity.*
He scolds, but eventually
Leads you into the open.
(Rumi, "The Core of Masculinity,"
lines 3–11)

One can already hear the howls of protest from a culture that is blind to dark light, that has no capacity for seeing in dark light. In this regard, Ron Schenk's book rightfully disturbs the soul. No trite formulas here! No subservient bow to conventional wisdom! No Dr. Phil! Just the simple statement of the ways things are when we do not stay in the bright, shadowless light of the noonday sun too long. Schenk's book is an antidote to heat stroke, and lest the reader miss the point of Rumi's poem, he follows it with a poem from Rilke, which shows another darker side of the relation between fathers and sons (73; Bly et al. 1992):

Sometimes a man stands up
*   during supper*
and walks outdoors, and keeps
*   on walking,*
because of a church that stands
*   somewhere in the East.*
And his children say blessings on
*   him as if he were dead.*
And another man, who remains
*   inside his own house*
dies there, inside the dishes
and the glasses,
so that his children have to go
*   far out into the world*
toward the same church,
*   which he forgot.*
("Sometimes a Man Stands Up
During Supper")

Seeing in dark light is not politically correct!

The chapter on marriage is equally provocative. Even the title captures it: "The Torture of 'Real'tionships/The Rites of Marriage." The key theme in this chapter is that relationships are a third reality within which each finds through the other a path to self. Citing Plato to the effect that something in us always wants to go down, Schenk artfully describes how falling in love serves this desire. "The soul," he says, "finds a form, a relationship, to fill this need as a way of coming into its own essential nature" (2001, 94). Drawing on alchemy and its processes of *coagulatio* and *solutio,* Schenk shows how it is the relationship as a living third that questions the couple. Not what does each want from the other, but what the relationship wants is the issue. As in the fairy tale of the "Frog King," which he cites, "When we ask, 'What does it want'? we are coming nearer to addressing the life of the relationship itself" (100). To do so, of course, is to experience a sacrifice of the ego and its own narcissistic demands, a petit mort in everyday life. The high rate of divorce in contemporary culture is one way in which we are engaged in a flight from and denial of death.

"Part Four: Death as Visible" contains essays on "The Necessity of Violence" and "The Soul of Race/The Heart of Color." In the first essay, Schenk underscores how America's fantasies of innocence and virtue belie, for example, its own violent treatment of its native population. "Americans," he writes, "don't remember very well." Our national amnesia covers over how "...we are a culture of violence in history, attitudes, and belief systems, and in our use of violence as a means to wealth and power" (Schenk 2001, 121). To see in dark light, however, is to be against forgetting and all the essays in Schenk's book are in service to this work. Thus, the essay on

race calls us to remember "...raciality as difference ..." where raciality as distinct from racism acknowledges and respects ethnicity as a life world of experience, values, customs, and beliefs to be explored and validated (147). In this chapter, Schenk also considers the important contributions of Michael Vannoy Adams (1996) to the issue of depth psychology's own blindness to racism, and in the closing section on the heart of color, he reminds us that if we are to make any progress against racism, we will have "... to imagine not only ethnicity, but color, and especially the color black, in a different way" (149).

Ron Schenk closes his book with an Epilogue in which he briefly discusses the trial of O.J. Simpson and the death of Princess Diana. I will not, however, summarize them, trusting that I have given enough of the flavor of the style of this book and its content to excite the reader's imagination. This book is a good companion whose chapters are rich in content and written with an invitational style that welcomes the reader into the joy of thinking and imagination. In the end, I would add only that this book is also a rare blend of two traditions: Ron Schenk brings together phenomenology and Jungian psychology to create a depth psychology of the cultural world, which I describe as cultural therapeutics. And he does so without burdening his discourse with the jargon of either tradition. Read this book, perhaps with a good bottle of wine nearby, and certainly while outdoors. The book is about being in the world with eyes that can see in dark light.

BIBLIOGRAPHY

Adams, Michael Vannoy. 1996. *The Multicultural Imagination: "Race," Color and the Unconscious,* New York: Routledge.

Bly, Robert, James Hillman, and Michael
    Meade, eds. 1992. The Rag and Bone
    Shop of the Heart: Poems for Men.
    New York: Harper Collins.

cummings, e. e. 1954. 100 Selected Poems.
    New York: Grove Press.

Romanyshyn, Robert. 1989/2000. Tech-
    nology As Symptom and Dream.
    London and New York: Routledge.

Schenk, Ronald. 2001. Dark Light: The
    Appearance of Death in Everyday Life.
    Albany: State University
    of New York Press.

ABSTRACT
ROBERT ROMANYSHYN. 2007. "Seeing in
the Dark Light of the Soul." JUNG JOURNAL:
CULTURE & PSYCHE, 1:4, 76-81. Review of Ronald Schenk's *Dark Light: The Appearance of
Death in Everyday Life.* Albany: State University of New York Press, 2001. This book provides a fresh and compelling examination of
contemporary familial relationships and cultural forms, locating soul and shadow using
an engaging style and a theoretical weave of
phenomenology and Jungian psychology.

KEY WORDS
phenomenology, culture, shadow, trickster,
fathers and sons, soul, marriage, alchemy

Voices from the Well

Review of Dennis Slattery's *Harvesting Darkness: Essays on Literature, Myth, Film, and Culture* Lincoln, Nebraska: iUniverse, Inc. 2006

EVANS LANSING SMITH

*This selection of essays spans the course of a most productive career, and it
will be invaluable to all of us interested in myth, literature, film, composition
theory, poetry, and culture seen through the lens of an accomplished archetypalist. Dennis Slattery writes with graceful insight about a wide range of topics: Sophocles, Ovid, Dante, Melville, and Rilke; the films of Wim Wenders;
the problem of violence in our culture; the soul-making dynamics of wounded
bodies; and the application of mythical models to the writing process. Hence, the
book's wide ranging appeal — to healthcare professionals, theologians, philosophers, analysts of both Freudian and Jungian persuasions, poets and teachers of
writing, mythologists, and film and literary critics.*

The Jungian fascination with the
tension between and union of opposites
serves Slattery well as an organizing and
thematic principle in several of these
exquisite essays. Indeed, the notion of what
Jung called the *Mysterium coniunctionis*
(the reconciliation of opposites as the
fulfillment of the alchemical process of
individuation) followed upon the Hegelian
dialectic of the nineteenth century, a

EVANS LANSING SMITH is Professor of English at Midwestern State University, in
Wichita Falls, Texas, and Adjunct Professor of Mythological Studies at the Pacifica
Graduate Institute in California. He is the author of eight books and numerous articles on
comparative literature and mythology. His most recent book, *Postmodern Magus: Myth
and Poetics in the Work of James Merrill,* is forthcoming from The University of Iowa Press.
Correspondence: 3410 Taft, Wichita Falls, TX 76308, USA.

dialectic one can trace all the way from Hegel to Schopenhauer, Goethe, Wagner, Nietzsche, and on to Freud and Jung. In Slattery's book, a variety of polarities runs through the collection, conferring unity upon the whole: the dialectics of spirit and matter, *civitas* and *communitas, kairos* and *kronos,* weave in and out of the individual essays, forming the warp and woof of a lovely tapestry. We find, for example, that the angel in Wim Wender's film, *Wings of Desire,* becomes more spiritual by being wounded and thus more fully incarnated in the material world; that Dante delicately balances the divine incarnation of Christ (*kairos*) with the dynamics of human history (*kronos*) in which that revelation must occur; and that, in Melville's *Moby Dick* (a special favorite of Slattery's), the crew of the Pequod moves from a soul-less *civitas,* dominated by mercantile concerns, to a genuine *communitas,* in which each finds meaning in connection to the other members of the group. Because the crew is of diverse ethnicity, a multicultural community emerges, indeed a global society — hence the novel's continued relevance to our contemporary dilemma.

Another central concern of the book is the reflection upon certain key myths and texts as metaphors of what I call in my own books *poeisis* and *hermeneusis* — that is to say, the creative mysteries of writing and interpretation. As a lifelong teacher of rhetoric and poetry, Slattery joins a small handful of archetypal critics interested in mythical models for composition and interpretation of texts. Randolph Severson, for example, applied the myth of Eros and Psyche to the dynamic mysteries of reading and interpretation — Psyche the soul buried in the text, the object of the reader's quest, driven by Eros. Slattery moves in a different direction, offering a fascinating analysis of the myth of Echo and Narcissus as presented in Ovid, in which the pool Narcissus gazes into is a blank page for a reflective composition on the theme of love and death. In his essay on Melville, Slattery turns (as I, too, have in my books) to the myth of the descent to the underworld as a metaphor for the creative mysteries of the writing and reading of a text. More generally, Slattery cogently applies the myth of descent and return (which Homer called the *nekyia*) to the popular science-fiction film *Aliens* (in which he brilliantly finds the myth of Demeter and Persephone), to John Keats's "Ode to a Nightingale," and to Wim Wenders' film *Wings of Desire.* In so doing, Slattery emphasizes the continued flexibility and presence of this most ancient of myths in even the most recent manifestations of popular culture.

Seeing old things in new ways, and seeing new things from the perspective of the old, is Slattery's magic trick — one executed with the grace of a master archetypalist, teacher, and poet, one who has honed his craft through a lifetime of disciplined, committed achievement. How many of us get all the major work of the day done before six in the morning, rising early enough to do so before taking on the tasks of the day? For Slattery, these tasks involve the incredibly rigorous and productive schedule of teaching in the Mythological Studies Program of the Pacifica Graduate Institute, lecturing all over the country to a wide range of audiences, and gathering us all together by reaching out to form creative connections that span the continent and abroad, bringing international groups into the orbit of his contribution.

As Louise Cowan notes in the Foreword, Dennis Slattery's collection is to be celebrated for its "wide competence in multiple modes of thought," and for the "poetic universe" (2006, i) in which the work is grounded. It will open new doors for those long involved in the related fields of myth, psychology, art history (there is a beautiful essay on Rodin), and literature, and serve well as a lovely introduction to those just starting out. In the long run, perhaps the two groups — precursor and ephebe, *senex* and *puer* — are one.

BIBLIOGRAPHY

Aliens. 1986. Screenplay by James Cameron, David Giler, and Walter Hill. Directed by James Cameron.

Ovid. 1980. "Echo and Narcissus." *The Metamorphoses of Ovid.* Trans. A. E. Watts. San Francisco: North Point Press.

Keats, John. 1973. "Ode to a Nightingale." *Keats: Poetical Works.* Ed. H. W. Garrod. London and Oxford: OxfordUniversity Press.

Melville, Herman. 1979. *Moby Dick.* Berkeley: University of California Press.

Slattery, Dennis. 2006. *Harvesting Darkness: Essays on Literature, Myth, Film, and Culture.* New York: iUniverse, Inc.

Wings of Desire (Himmel über Berlin). 1987. Screenplay by Wim Wenders and Peter Handke. Directed by Wim Wenders.

ABSTRACT

EVANS LANSING SMITH. 2007. "Voices from the Well," Review of Dennis Slattery's *Harvesting Darkness: Essays on Literature, Myth, Film, and Culture.* iUniverse, Inc., 2006. JUNG JOURNAL: CULTURE & PSYCHE, 1:4, 81-83.

KEY WORDS

alchemy, echo, descent, ethnicity, film, Keats, Melville, *Mysterium coniunctionis, nekyia,* Ovid, poetry, race, soul

Luigi Zoja: Cultivating the Soul

Luigi Zoja's *Cultivating the Soul.*
London: Free Association, 2005.

STEVEN B. HERRMANN

Némesis and *Hýbris* According to Zoja

In preparation for this review of Luigi Zoja's book Cultivating the Soul, *I turned to his earlier published works in search of a guiding notion. To my surprise, I found it in* Growth and Guilt *(1995a): Némesis—the ancient Greek goddess associated with the woods* (nemos), *man's inborn sense of shame* (aidos), *and law* (nomos). *In Zoja's view, we need Némesis to keep us in balance. Némesis is an image for the human psyche. If we listen to her, she carries the capacity to nourish us; if not, she may strike us down with a vengeance. Zoja defines Némesis as "distributive justice moved by the anger of the gods, by which*

STEVEN B. HERRMANN, Ph.D., MFT, is a candidate in advanced training at the C.G. Jung Institute of San Francisco. He is the author of "Melville's Vision of Evil," published in *The San Francisco Jung Institute Library Journal* (22:3, 2003), and of papers dealing with such diverse topics as American poetry, shamanism, slavery and race, transformation, and psychological trauma. *Correspondence:* 2220 Mountain Blvd., Suite 240, Oakland, CA., 94611. USA. (510) 531-2534. sbherrmann@comcast.net.

any person is inevitably cut down to size" (2005, 170). By "inevitably," Zoja is referring to the process of individuation: no one is free from the individuating "curse" of Némesis.

A second linked notion is that of overweening pride (*hýbris*). The Greeks were terrified of *hýbris*. Originally viewed as a type of violence stemming from the passions, *hýbris* is similar to Jung's idea of inflation. Zoja points out that Jung was the first to view *hýbris* psychologically (1995a, 179). In this review, I will focus on the relationship between *hýbris* and Némesis in Zoja's writings within the context of a story from the *Odyssey,* in which Zoja presents the story of Odysseus's homecoming as an analytical narrative for our times.

In "September 11: Transatlantic Reflections," Zoja writes that in the ancient Greek drama *hýbris* is inseparable from *Némesis* (2002, 19); the two notions are psychologically interconnected. Whereas *hýbris* is unavoidable in the process of psychological development, Némesis helps keep inflation in check. Today, the problem of inflation has reached titanic proportions, impacting all aspects of culture. The need for new myths to help check human *hýbris* is correspondingly great. In a similar vein, Zoja says that the story of Divine Justice in Hebrew scripture "screams out to be retold. Under these circumstances the latent myth of punishment for divine arrogance (*némesis* punishing *hýbris*) combines with a genuine need for Divine Justice" (2002, 21). Zoja is zeroing in on a psychological law that is built into the very fabric of the world. Of all the human passions, he says, *hýbris* is the most treacherous. It is the "arrogance that makes us blind, or, more precisely, that which makes us incapable of perceiving the proportions and limits of everything human. *Hýbris* is the only sin, moreover, which is common to all religions" (2005, 205). The Greek word *hýbris* recurs throughout all of Zoja's major books and

papers. Although many of the great world religions, such as Judaism, Christianity, Buddhism, and Islam, have offered answers to the problem of inflation, Zoja feels that analysis is "one of the very few antidotes to modern *hýbris*" (2005, 214).

The Therapeutic Need for Tragic Narratives

Analysis, as a discipline of knowledge, Zoja tells us, descended from an "ancient ancestor: the tradition of tragic narrative" (2005, 195). For Zoja, true (tragic) narratives are necessary for psychotherapists and analysts as well as for culture generally; for without narratives, psychic life cannot be perceived as unfolding beneath the aegis of myth. The great teacher of life, Zoja argues, is tragic drama; the aim of epic poetry is to administer a dose of moral consciousness, a sense of moderation, and an awareness of proper limitations. In this sense, Zoja finds the myths of ancient Greece to be the richest and most meaningful (93), particularly the Homeric poems, the *Iliad* and *Odyssey* (probably dating from the eighth century BCE): "history and myth; the gods and men; matter and spirit; ethics and aesthetics" (116). Zoja loves the Greek classics. He sees Homer as perhaps the greatest bard who has ever lived, maintaining that "in spite of the mammoth conquests of the centuries that followed Homer, no form of culture continued to be able to address itself to the growth of the whole individual" (119). As a tragic poet, Homer exemplifies the poet's task. Embodying the wisdom of the Self within Western history, he makes us conscious of warlike passions, moral principles, and erotic impulses, and connects us to our most vital human instincts.

How have we lost touch with this Homeric wholeness of character? This is, Zoja maintains, a "problem of knowledge" (2005, 203). In his reflections on Sophocles' Oedipus Rex, for instance, he writes that in the beginning of that tale, "Tiresias, the wise man is blind: blind and limited"; in the end, Oedipus, too, is blind. Having achieved the limits of knowledge, the limits of his development have brought him to a "form of natural wisdom" (204). The solution to the problem of knowledge — the sin of consciousness that came to humanity from the temptation of the serpent in Hebrew myth — may be found in the great epics of tragedy that infuse suffering and wisdom. Wisdom is born only out of great anguish and pain.

Placing more value on wisdom than on knowledge, Zoja returns to the primary concern of philosophical investigation since the Renaissance, arguing that "the state of pain and laceration...[is]...part of the soul's original condition" (2005, 199). By going back to the wisdom literature of the ancient Greeks, he attempts to teach us a way to assimilate the achievement of the Greeks through tragic reflections — that is, by puncturing our sense of pride. Our pride, in other words, is destined to be lacerated, to be punctured by a lance. Némesis helps keep our inflation in check by lancing our egos and infusing us with shame both on a personal and a cultural level; tragic narratives and truthful relationships (such as that experienced in analysis) may be one of the most effective ways to achieve this end.

When we think of the centrality of tragic narratives within the context of analysis, it becomes apparent that we all need to tell and to hear painful stories. Are not stories of childhood trauma, broken relationships, or failures in the workplace forms of tragic narrative that keep us humble? Such stories are food for the soul, creating pathways to greater awareness through the purgation of affects such as fear, pity, and sorrow; their bitterness and tears help us reverse the tragic situation (peripeteia) in order to arrive at a recognition (*anagnorisis* or a change from ignorance to knowledge) that may bring relief and joy. Zoja helps us understand that the soul needs tragedy to tell the truth.

Suffering — life's first condition — comes to us through the awareness of death. Death, in the writings of the Greek tragedians, imparts the mighty lesson of the relativity of all earthly things, thus becoming a source of a transcendental wisdom. "Today," declares Zoja "the very word [Death] is avoided, and everything that might call it to mind is rejected or repressed" (2005, 185). Death is the great ethical teacher because it reminds us how we stay free of *hýbris* — for death is ultimately inseparable from life.

Homecoming

Through his reading of Homer's Odyssey, Zoja arrives at a psychological rendering of the text that does poetic, as well as analytic, justice to an old myth. In Zoja's masterful retelling of the story, he sees Odysseus as a violent, yet admirable father figure, a structure of the Self that knows how to transform the passion of *hýbris* into a psychological awareness of limits. The myth of Odysseus is, in Zoja's view, "the prototype for the men of the Western world, both ancient and modern" (2001, 98). Rather than a sign of outer warlike conquest, Zoja interprets Odysseus as a "symbol of discovery" (2001, 101): a way of seeing and relating to the world that is capable of balancing power with moderation (1995a, 181) — Zoja's theory in a nutshell.

After an arduous journey home following the Trojan War, Odysseus finds the vile suitors of Ithaca contending for his wife Penelope's hand at his palace and responds with an inner sense of retributive justice. Zoja returns to this story in several of his books: "Hidden beneath the rags of the beggar we in fact will find Odysseus, and the chieftains of Ithaca are to feel the brunt of his arrows as the agent of their final *némesis*" (1995a, 49) and "The whole of the Odyssey is permeated with a warning and appeal: woe to those who forget the land of the fathers!" (2001, 107).

Zoja's Odysseus symbolizes a quality of consciousness, desperately needed in our times, that can string a sturdy psychological "bow." By plucking the bow's string to produce a lyrical music, Odysseus sounds the keynote for the transformation of consciousness within Western culture: the music of analysis. Few of us as yet in our culture have learned to pluck this string, lacking as we do the emotional resilience or the metaphorical lyrical capacity embodied in the Odysseus image.

Odysseus's violence presents us with a slightly different problem. Standing up to the nobles of the kingdom of Ithaca who threaten his marriage bed, Odysseus's aggression symbolizes a retributive justice, a powerful masculine instinct that fiercely defends his inner union with his soulmate, Penelope. Odysseus's marriage bed is an inner palace where the *coniunctio* with his anima-wife takes place. As long as men continue to perpetuate the cycle of violence, they miss the psychological meaning of Némesis. Like Telemachus, Odysseus's son, we need to re-enter Odysseus's palace and string the bow in *imagination:*

Telemachus lives in a state of suspension and waiting: not so much for a real person — of whom he has no memory, and who departed when he was still

in swaddling clothes — but for an *image of* the father, a noble image he might admire. (2001, 107)

In my psychotherapy practice, I have heard countless variations on this theme of the son waiting for his father. Time and again, I have been witness to boys and girls in latency and adolescence who express a longing to see, know, and admire their father. In the transference, they seek their father's appearance in their lives. They are looking for new metaphors of the father that can infuse them with life. Often I have seen a direct correlation between the absence of the father in a boy's or a girl's life and outbursts of incipient violence. Here, my task has been to engage such youngsters in a process of reflecting through narratives about their tragic feelings surrounding their father-loss and their anger over the fact that they do not have a stable image of a strong father-presence to support them from within.

In Zoja's view, Odysseus is the inner image of the boy's emotional longing. As we know, the inner image must be awakened (as in a mirror) through an outer relationship with a man, or for a woman, through the father archetype in the transference. When Odysseus left for Troy, Telemachus was a mere babe in his father's arms, marking the beginning of twenty long years of waiting. This corresponds roughly to the developmental age when the "wisdom factor" in the unconscious — the feminine-relatedness function — is activated by a paternal role model (real or transferential), releasing instinctive knowledge from the young person's unconscious regarding the nature of his or her calling. It is interesting to note that Telemachus receives his first instructions about becoming a man from a feminine deity, the goddess Athena, the guardian-deity of Athens and patroness of Western civilization. According to myth, the warrior goddess was born without a mother, fully armored, out of Zeus' forehead. A single-parent goddess dedicated to the heroic principle of vocation for women and men, she counsels acts of strategy rather than physical violence in order to skillfully reach the goals of one's calling. Although Athena, together with the goddess Hera, launched the Trojan War following the Judgment of Paris, her unique affection for Odysseus led her to mentor Telemachus, advising him to leave home and seek out news of his father's existence. Boys and girls who have been raised without a father often decry the lack of such a mentoring figure, which can, however, be activated in the unconscious through a relationship to an analyst.

Odysseus's solution to the problem of separation, both from his son Telemachus and from his wife Penelope, might be summed up in a single word: homecoming. Odysseus "holds firm within himself to a single, primary purpose: returning to his home" (2001, 102). The home Zoja is speaking about here is not the literal Ithaca of ancient Greece; it is a great primordial symbol of the hearth, the goddess Hestia, present within us all (1995a, 164). In *The Father,* Zoja constructs an image of the father who is both grounded and real, aware of aggression and yet compassionate.

An Ethic of the Reappearance of Natural Limits

In Zoja's mind, Western cultures that have been waiting for the father's return will only be able to live in harmony with themselves and the rest of the world if they subject themselves to an ethical principle in which natural limits are allowed to make their claims on us (1995a, 171; 183). Without a sense of Némesis's limits, we forsake the Earth, fail to respect our fellow creatures, and remain blind in our ecological awareness. We need tragic narratives to help us stay true to nature's primal wisdom and the human heart's compassionate stirrings. The myth of Odysseus presented by Zoja — particularly for boys and men — addresses a glaring weakness: the failure to recognize our ecological *hýbris.* Odysseus' homecoming represents a change of heart, away from a path of outer destruction toward one of relatedness centered in the wisdom of the Earth and soul.

Paideía

Zoja says that the Telemachia (the story of the orphan son's voyage away from his mother Penelope in search of Odysseus was probably added after the rest of the Odyssey was completed (2001, 109–110). Following this lead, Zoja shows how the narrative continues to unfold in our inner quest for the father in analysis and culture. Telemachus's discovery of maturity and his longing for the father survives in Zoja's mythic and psychological vision of *paideía,* the "inner culture" of the soul, or cultura animi.

Zoja's aim in *Cultivating the Soul* is to show us how Telemachus's passage into adulthood "reveals the need for a realization of natural potential to be an innate and archetypal ideal" (2005, 91). Oftentimes for therapy this means that the father will need to be evoked in the transference in both its light and dark forms. So often in our culture, fathers are unable to maintain a healthy tension between love and aggression. The Homeric poems show us how to convert the impulse of sex and aggression into healthy forms of relational Eros mediated through the feeling function. Athena's mirror is an image of transformation that makes such mediation possible. Athena awarded this reflecting shield to Perseus to crown his victory over Medusa. Athena's mirror can help us reflect on our own malevolence to get a more objective, self-critical view of ourselves. This is the poet's as well as the analyst's job.

The analyst, like the poet, is a storyteller. Arguing like a tragedian, Zoja laments: "our culture's loss of the idea of *paideía* has induced a vacuum that sooner or later had to be filled with the Jungian idea of individuation, or with other forms of acculturative consciousness (such as the Oriental philosophies)" (2005, 123). But then Zoja calls for optimism:

> If we manage to retrieve the true and original meaning of the idea of culture, we will also be able to assert that every culture encourages, to a lesser or greater degree, the individual's tendency to realize personal potential, and thus to effect the process we refer to as individuation. (93)

In analytic work, *paideía* is constellated intersubjectively by nurturing those seeds that are planted by *physis* (nature) and are thus latent in the transference/countertransference relationship, but which are "incapable of germination without adequate cultivation (culture)" (2005, 101). To cultivate these germs, the modern analyst needs to stay attuned to the transformative power of Eros that effects changes in the intersubjective analytical consciousness. The story of Odysseus is an Eros narrative — in Zoja's view the master analytic narrative. The tale contains an image of the transformation of consciousness that takes place in the *vas bene claussum* of Odysseus's palace. In Odysseus's palace, a *"cultura animi,"* which is the culture of cultivation of the soul" (97), takes place, a *coniunctio* between Penelope, Odysseus, and Telemachus that

is simultaneously in the world and of the world (98).

Zoja calls our attention to a "diffuse nostalgia" for that part of culture that is "internal" and potentially also external, linking us to the world soul, or *Anima Mundi* (2005, 98). This form of Eros is more than desire and has the capacity for scrupulous self-scrutiny. Narration is one way to bring self-critical Eros into reality. Zoja chooses Odysseus's palace as a metaphor for this process: "Ulysses' palace is a recent, fragile construct and has to be regenerated through continuing to construct it" (2001, 109; Ulysses is the Roman name for Odysseus). By reviving Odysseus's palace as a living symbol for a place of self-observation, Zoja regenerates its potential reality for his readers. Self-scrutiny includes the possibility of seeing our inner potential for violence. In fact, the same story, if read "semiotically" as a sign calling for literal imitation, can have disastrous consequences, perpetuating a cycle of violence devoid of Eros.

Zoja's writings remind us, in fact, that the "genocidal tide that the Greeks set in motion" has become the tragedy of our current civilization (2001, 83). Unconsciously, we are living the myth of the Trojan War all over again. This is why reading tragic narratives about the father's homecoming are so important for us today. By returning to such stories, we come to see how we got to where we are now. This is *paideía*.

Building on such stories within the temenos of analysis can help to make the archetypes of sex, aggression, and spirit conscious in the transference. "We know that the search for the father is more than a material necessity; it is also a universal psychological need. All of us, like Telemachus, want to know whose child we are" (2001, 285). The story of Telemachus's fate as an orphan can be deeply transformative when it is retold analytically by a master storyteller, and when this occurs during a time of kairos — "the right moment — for a 'metamorphosis of the gods'" (Jung CW 10, ¶585) — new meanings can come to us.

When we can mourn or express anger over the loss of admirable images of the father, doorways open for new narratives. Archetypes of culture may then provide us with an experiential understanding of tragic awareness. Greek tragedy has a great deal to teach us in this regard, as do Zoja's renderings of tragic narratives from a psychological point of view. For Zoja "happy endings" tend to avoid the suffering that we need for our individuation. Notions of happy endings forget the wisdom that comes from antiquity, just as they forget the lessons that come from the experience of analysis itself. Only concerned with overcoming pain, they become measures of repression — with the disastrous consequences with which we have become so familiar in our times. One wonders if the next millennium will lack all awareness of tragic sentiment (2005, 212).

Recalling the history of one of Greek tragedy's mythical figures — Odysseus — Zoja helps us maintain a sense of an ancient wisdom born of reflection. In pursuit of consciousness, Zoja preserves a "paternal function" for analysis and culture, calling us to reacquaint ourselves with our fathers' past (2001, 298–299). This quest is common to epic poetry and to analysis (1995b, 2007). By reading the story of Telemachus's father-loss and empathically feeling into his pain and longing for his father's return home, we can come to recognize the symptom of father-absence as a "companion," which may accompany the very transformation that the analyst aught to facilitate (2005, 69).

Conclusion

In concluding this review, I would like to say how much Zoja's reflections on *némesis* and *hýbris* have helped me track the threads of tragedy, the ethics of natural limits, and *paideía* in my own psychotherapeutic work. It is remarkable how central tragic narratives are to our therapeutic transference-countertransference dialectic with patients, particularly in the father-son and father-daughter relational dynamics. The primal longing for the father's homecoming, whether the father has been present or absent in a person's life, appears to be at the heart of analytic work. The need to weave tragic narratives around father-son and father-daughter reunion is part of the psyche's natural language — its calling to express itself in the form of bittersweet music. As a poet and a psychotherapist, I listen for the keynote of tragedy in the soul of my patients, where something cracks in the voice and an affect-image of grief, rage, or sorrow quickens in a place of *cultura animi*. There is a primal longing in children, adolescents, and adults to frame their suffering in metaphors and story. I have found this to be especially true in my work with children who lost a parent at an early age to divorce or who were orphaned in infancy. And not infrequently, I have found that the leitmotif of tragedy has arisen in dream, sandplay, or imagination to form a master narrative for that child's transformation and healing.

By plucking the string of his bow, Zoja recalls Homer's lyrics of tragedy, chanted in iambic pentameter, to teach us the painful lessons of war so crucial in our time. Holding up the reflecting shield of Athena, he helps us make the impulse of violence conscious. Most importantly, he shows us that new images of the father are needed in society that may transform our lives.

BIBLIOGRAPHY

Jung, C.G. 1957. "The Undiscovered Self." CW 10, ¶585).

Zoja, Luigi. 1995a. *Growth and Guilt: Psychology and the Limits of Development.* London: Routledge.

——. 1995b. "Reflections Concerning Ethics." In *Cast the First Stone: Ethics in Analytic Practice.* Willmette: Chiron.

——. 2001. *The Father: Historical, Psychological and Cultural Perspectives.* London: Bruner-Routledge.

——. 2002. "September 11: Transatlantic Reflections." In *Jungian Reflections on September 11.* Einseideln: Daimon Verlag.

——. 2005. *Cultivating the Soul.* London: Free Association.

——. 2007. *Ethics and Analysis.* College Station: Texas A & M University.

ABSTRACT

STEVEN B. HERRMANN. 2007. "Luigi Zoja: Cultivating the Soul." Review of Luigi Zoja, *CultivatingtheSoul.* London:FreeAssociation London,2005, JUNG JOURNAL: CULTURE & PSYCHE, 1:4, 83-90. The author follows an interconnected thread between the notions of *Némesis* and *hýbris* in Luigi Zoja's major books and papers. Herrmann argues that for Zoja, true (tragic) narratives are necessary for psychotherapists and analysts as well as for culture generally; for without narratives, psychic life cannot be perceived as unfolding beneath the ægis of myth. The great teacher of life, Zoja asserts, is tragic drama; the aim of epic poetry is to infuse a dose of moral consciousness, a sense of moderation, and an awareness of proper limitations. Through Zoja's reading of Homer's *Odyssey,* Herrmann introduces Zoja's psychological rendering of the text, a reading that does poetic, as well as analytic, justice to an old myth. In Zoja's masterful retelling, Odysseus can be seen as a violent, yet admirable father figure, a structure of the Self that knows how to transform the passion of *hýbris* into a psychological awareness of limits. As long as men continue to perpetuate the cycle of violence, they will miss the psychological meaning of Némesis. The story of Odysseus is an Eros narrative — nothing less than the master analytic narrative. The story contains an image of the transformation of consciousness that takes place in Odysseus's palace. In Odysseus's palace, a *cultura animi*, or culture of cultivation of the soul, takes place — a *coniunctio* between Penelope, Odysseus, and Telemachus — that is simultaneously in and of the world. By reading the story of Telemachus's father-loss and empathically feeling into his pain and longing for his father's return home, we can come to recognize the symptom of father-absence as a companion that may accompany the very transformation the analyst needs to facilitate. Most importantly, Zoja shows us that new images of the father are needed in society.

KEY WORDS

Zoja, Odyssey, Odysseus, *paideía, cultura animi, hýbris,* Némesis, tragic narrative, divine justice.

BOOKS RECEIVED JANUARY–SEPTEMBER 2007

Jung Journal's Editors gratefully acknowledge the receipt of these many fine books as review copies. All books are considered for review and are donated to the C.G. Jung Institute of San Francisco Library.

We encourage our readers to examine this list and to submit reviews of these books. Reviews may be as short as a page or a longer article that considers more than one book and/or a subject area in depth.

Akhtar, Salman, ed. 2007. *Listening to Others: Developmental and Clinical Aspects of Empathy and Attunement.* Lanham, MD: Jason Aronson.

Alayarian, Aida. 2007. *Resilience, Suffering and Creativity: The Work of the Refugee Therapy Centre.* London: Karnac Books.

Aldridge, David and Jorg Fachner, eds. 2006. *Music and Altered States: Consciousness, Transcendence, Therapy and Addictions.* Philadelphia, PA: Jessica Kingsley Publishers.

Anderson, Frances Sommer. 2007. *Bodies in Treatment: The Unspoken Dimension.* New York: The Analytic Press.

Appiah, Kwame Anthony. 2007. *The Ethics of Identity.* Princeton, NJ: Princeton University Press.

Archer, Ruth, ed. 2006. *Dual Realities: Counseling and Psychotherapy with People with Serious Physical Illness* and *Disability: The Search for Meaning in the Therapeutic Space.* London: Karnac Books.

Ariadne, Patricia. 2006. *Women Dreaming-into-Art.* Lakeville, MN: Galde Press Inc.

Ashton, Paul W. 2007. *From the Brink: Experiences of the Void from a Depth Psychology Perspective.* London: Karnac Books.

Austin, Sue. 2005. *Women's Aggressive Fantasies: A Post-Jungian Exploration of Self-Hatred, Love and Agency.* New York: Routledge.

Aziz, Robert. 2007. *The Syndetic Paradigm: The Untrodden Path Beyond Freud and Jung.* Albany, NY: State University of New York Press.

Boulanger, Ghislaine. 2007. *Wounded by Reality: Understanding and Treating Adult Onset Trauma.* New York: The Analytic Press.

Boyd-Franklin, Nancy. 2006. *Black Families in Therapy.* New York: Guilford Press.

Breitenberger, Barbara. 2004. *Aphrodite & Eros: The Development of Erotic Mythology in Greek Poetry and Cult.* New York: Routledge.

Briggs, Andrew, ed. 2006. *Surviving Space: Papers on Infant Observation.* London: Karnac Books.

Brodie, Bruce R. 2007. *Adolescence and Delinquency: An Object Relations Theory Approach.* Lanham, MD: Jason Aronson.

Broom, Brian. 2007. *Meaning-Full Disease: How Personal Experience and Meanings Cause and Maintain Physical Illness.* London: Karnac Books.

Browning, Deborah L., ed. 2007. *Adolescent Identities: A Collection of Readings.* New York: The Analytic Press.

Bruzzi, Stella. 2006. *Bringing Up Daddy. Fatherhood and Masculinity in Postwar Hollywood.* London: British Film Institute.

Buren, Jane Van. 2007. *Mothers and Daughters and the Origins of Female Subjectivity.* New York: Routledge.

Burston, Daniel. 2007. *Erik Erikson and the American psyche: Ego, Ethics, and Evolution.* New York: Jason Aronson.

Casement, Ann and David Tacey. (2006). *The Idea of the Numinous: Contemporary Jungian and Psychoanalytic Perspectives.* New York: Routledge.

Chalquist, Craig. 2007. *Terrapsychology: Reengaging the Soul of Place.* New Orleans: Spring Journal Books.

Chireau, Yvonne P. 2006. *Black Magic: Religion and the African American Conjuring Tradition.* Berkeley, CA: University of California Press.

Christou, Evangelos. 2007. *The Logos of the Soul.* Putnam, CT: Spring Publications.

Cole, Peter, ed. 2007. *The Dream of the Poem: Hebrew Poetry from Muslim and Christian Spain, 950–1492.* Princeton, NJ: Princeton University Press.

Connelly, Joan Breton. 2007. *Portrait of a Priestess: Women and Ritual in Ancient Greece.* Princeton, NJ: Princeton University Press.

Cooper, Paul C., ed. 2007. *Into the Mountain Stream.* Lanham, MD: Jason Aronson.

Cope, Theo A. 2006. *Fear of Jung: The Complex Doctrine and Emotional Science.* London: Karnac Books.

Corbett, Lionel. 2006. *Psyche and the Sacred: Spirituality Beyond Religion.* New Orleans, LA: Spring Journal Books.

Costello, Melanie Starr. 2006. *Imagination, Illness and Injury: Jungian Psychology and the Somatic Dimensions of Perception.* New York: Routledge.

Currie, Billye B. 2007. *The Gambler: Romancing Lady Luck: a Jungian Exploration.* Toronto: Inner City Books.

Daitch, Carolyn. 2007. *Affect Regulation Toolbox: Practical and Effective Hypnotic Interventions for the Over-Reactive Client.* New York: W. W. Norton.

Dreyer, Elizabeth A. 2007. *Holy Power, Holy Presence: Rediscovering Medieval Metaphors for the Holy Spirit.* Mahwah, NJ: Paulist Press.

Elsner, Jas. 2007. *Roman eyes: Visuality and Subjectivity in Art and Text.* Princeton, NJ: Princeton University Press.

Farber, David, ed. 2007. *What They Think of Us: International Perceptions of the United States Since 9/11.* Princeton, NJ: Princeton University Press.

Feeney, Denis. 2007. *Caesar's Calendar: Ancient Time and the Beginnings of History.* Berkeley, CA: University of California Press.

Foster, Angela, Adrian Dickinson, Bernadine Bishop, Josephine Klein, eds. 2006. *Difference: An Avoided Topic in Practice.* London: Karnac Books.

Gaitanidis, Anastasios and Polona Curk, eds. 2007. *Narcissism: A Critical Reader.* London: Karnac Books.

Galton, Graeme, ed. 2006. *Touch Papers: Dialogues on Touch in the Psychoanalytic Space.* London: Karnac Books.

Gilbert, Paul and Kent G. Bailey, eds. 2000. *Genes on the Couch: Explorations in Evolutionary Psychotherapy.* Hove, East Sussex: Brunner-Routledge.

Gould, Laurence, et al. 2007. *The Systems: Psychodynamics of Organization.* London: Karnac Books.

Hart, Onno van der, Ellert R. S. Nuenhuis, and Kathy Steele. 2006. *The Haunted Self: Structural Dissociation and the Treatment of Chronic Traumatization.* New York: W. W. Norton.

Hauke, Christopher. 2005. *Human Being Human: Culture and the Soul.* New York: Routledge.

Heath, Richard. 2007. *Sacred Number and the Origins of Civilization. The Unfolding of History Through the Mystery of Number.* Rochester, VT: Inner Traditions.

Hedges, Lawrence E. 2007. *Facing the Challenge of Liability in Psychotherapy Practice: Practicing Defensively.* New York: Jason Aronson.

Hill, Michael Ortiz with Mandaza Augustine Kandemwa. 2006. *The Village of the Water Spirits: the Dreams of African Americans.* Putnam, CT: Spring Publications.

Hillman, James. 2004. *City and Soul,* Uniform Ed., vol. 2. Putnam, CT: Spring Publications.

Hillman, James. 2007. *Mythic Figures.* Putnam, CT: Spring Publications.

Hillman, James. 2005. *Senex and Puer.* Putnam, CT: Spring Publications.

Josselson, Ruthellen. 2007. *Playing Pygmalion.* Lanham, MD: Jason Aronson.

Kluger, Rivkah and Yehezkel Kluger. 1990. *Remembering Jung,* No. 13. Los Angeles: C.G. Jung Institute of Los Angeles.

Kogan, Ilany. 2007. *The Struggle Against Mourning.* Lanham, MD: Jason Aronson.

Kradin, Richard. 2006. *The Herald Dream: An Approach to Dream Interpretation and the Implications of Initial Dreams in Psychotherapy.* London: Karnac Books.

Kramer, Milton. 2006. *The Dream Experience: A Systematic Exploration.* New York: Routledge.

Lanyado, Monica, ed. 2006. *A Question of Technique: Independent Psychoanalytic Approaches with Children and Adolescents.* New York: Routledge.

Lopez-Corvo, Rafael. 2006. *Wild Thoughts Searching for a Thinker: A Clinical Application of W. R. Bion's Theories.* London: Karnac Books.

Major, John S., ed. 2006. *The Three Boys and Other Buddhist Folktales from Tibet.* Honolulu, HI: University of Hawaii Press.

Mathews, Mel. 2006. *LeRoi.* Carmel, CA: Fisher King Press.

Mathews, Mel. 2006. *Menopause Man.* Carmel, CA: Fisher King Press.

Mathews, Mel. 2006. *SamSara.* Carmel, CA: Fisher King Press.

Mayes, Linda, ed. 2007. *Developmental Science and Psychoanalysis: Integration and Innovation.* London: Karnac Books.

McGoldrick, Monica, Joe Giordano, Joe, and John Pearce, eds. 2005. *Ethnicity and Family Therapy.* New York: Guilford Press.

Mehl-Madrona, Lewis. 2007. *Narrative Medicine: The Use of History and Story in the Healing Process.* Rochester, VT: Bear & Company.

Meissner, William W. 2007. *Time, Self, and Psychoanalysis.* Lanham, MD: Jason Aronson.

Merkur, Dan. 2007. *Crucified with Christ: Meditation on the Passion, Mystical Death, and the Medieval Invention of Psychotherapy.* Albany, NY: State University of New York Press.

Miller, David L. 2005. *Christs: Meditations on Archetypal Images in Christian Theology.* New Orleans, LA: Spring Journal Books.

Morley, Robert. 2007. *The Analysand's Tale.* London: Karnac Books.

Muller, John P. and Jane G. Tillman, eds. 2007. *The Embodied Subject.* Lanham, MD: Jason Aronson.

Newton, Lara. 2007. *Brothers and Sisters: Discovering the Psychology of Companionship.* New Orleans, LA: Spring Journal Books.

Novick, Kerry Kelly and Jack Novick. 2006. *Good Goodbyes: Knowing How to End in Psychotherapy and Psychoanalysis.* Lanham, MD: Jason Aronson.

Nunez, Luis Manuel. 2001. *Santeria Stories.* Putnam, CT: Spring Publications, Inc.

Oakes, Maud. 1990. *Remembering Jung.* No. 19. Los Angeles: C. G. Jung Institute of Los Angeles.

Page, Scott E. 2006. *The Difference. How the Power of Diversity Creates Better Groups, Firms, Schools, and Societies.* Princeton, NJ: Princeton University Press.

Pallaro, Patrizia, ed. 2007. *Authentic Movement: Moving the Body, Moving the Self, Being Moved: A Collection of Essays,* Vol. 2. Philadelphia, PA: Jessica Kingsley Publishers.

Parens, Henri, Afaf Mahfouz, Stuart W. Twemlow, and David E. Scharff, eds. 2007. *The Future of Prejudice: Psychoanalysis and the Prevention of Prejudice.* Lanham, MD: Rowman & Littlefield.

Paris, Ginette. 2007. *The Psychology of Abortion.* New York: Spring Publications.

Parnell, Laurel. 2006. *A Therapist's Guide to EMDR: Tools and Techniques for Successful Treatment.* New York: W. W. Norton.

Pascoe, C. J. 2007. *Dude, You're a Fag: Masculinity and Sexuality in High School.* Berkeley, CA: University of California Press.

Patterson, JoEllen, A. Ari Albala, Margaret E. McCahill, and Todd M. Edwards. 2006. *The Therapist's Guide to Psychopharmacology: Working with Patients, Families, and Physicians to Optimize Care.* New York: Guilford Press.

Peacher, Georgiana. 2006. *Skryabin Mysterium: Dream Mind of Alexander Scriabin.* Philadelphia, PA: Xlibris.

Peters, F. E. 2007. *The Voice, the Word, the Books: the Sacred Scripture of the Jews, Christians, and Muslims.* Princeton, NJ: Princeton University Press.

Petrucelli, Jean, ed. 2006. *Longing: Psychoanalytic Musings on Desire.* London: Karnac Books.

Piers, Craig, John P. Muller, and Joseph Brent, eds. 2007. *Self-Organizing Complexity in Psychological Systems.* Lanham, MD: Jason Aronson.

Quispel, Gilles. 1990. *Remembering Jung,* No. 18. Los Angeles: C. G. Jung Institute of Los Angeles.

Rangell, Leo. 2007. *The Road to Unity in Psychoanalytic Theory.* New York: Jason Aronson.

Richardson, Peter Tufts. 2007. *Archetype of the Spirit: Origins of Spirituality—Individual & Collective.* Rockland, ME: Red Barn Publishing.

Richo, David. 2007. *The Sacred Heart of the World: Restoring Mystical Devotion to Our Spiritual Life.* Mahwah, NJ: Paulist Press.

Rosen, Stephen Peter. 2007. *War and Human Nature*. Princeton, NJ: Princeton University Press.

Rowland, Susan. 2005. *Jung as a Writer*. Florence, KY: Routledge.

Schaverien, Joy, ed. 2006. *Gender, Countertransference and the Erotic Transference: Perspectives from Analytical Psychology and Psychoanalysis*. New York: Routledge.

Scholem, Gershom. 2006. *Alchemy and Kabbalah*. Putnam, CT: Spring Publications.

Seo, Audrey Yoshiko. 2007. *Enso: Zen Circle of Enlightenment*. Boston: Shambhala.

Sharp, Damian. 2006. *Simple Chinese Astrology*. Newburyport, MA: Conari Press.

Sharp, Daryl. 2007. *Eyes Wide Open: Late Thoughts (Another Jungian Romance)*. Toronto: Inner City Books.

Sharp, Daryl. 2006. *On Staying Awake: Getting Older and Bolder (Another Jungian Romance)*. Toronto: Inner City Books.

Slattery, Dennis Patrick. 2007. *A Limbo of Shards: Essays on Memory, Myth and Metaphor*. New York: iUniverse, Inc.

Sparks, J. Gary. 2007. *At the Heart of Matter: Synchronicity and Jung's Spiritual Testament*. Toronto: Inner City Books.

Stapley, Lionel F. 2006. *Individuals, Groups, and Organizations Beneath the Surface*. London: Karnac Books.

Stein, Murray. 2006. *The Principle of Individuation: Toward the Development of Human Consciousness*. New York: Chiron Publications.

Strickling, Bonnelle Lewis. 2007. *Dreaming About the Divine*. Albany, NY: State University of New York Press.

Tacey, David. 2007. *How to Read Jung*. London: W. W. Norton.

Tannen, Ricki Stefanie. 2007. *The Female Trickster: The Mask That Reveals: Post-Jungian and Postmodern Psychological Perspectives on Women in Contemporary Culture*. New York: Routledge.

Toro, Gianluca and Benjamin Thomas. 2007. *Drugs of the Dreaming: Oneirogens: Salvia Divinorum and Other Dream Enhancing Plants*. Rochester, VT: Park Street Press.

Tucker, William. 2007. *How People Change: The Short Story as Case History*. New York: Other Press.

Waddell, Terrie. 2006. *Mis/takes: Archetype, Myth and Identity in Screen Fiction*. New York: Routledge.

Walsh, Roger. 2007. *The World of Shamanism: New Views of an Ancient Tradition*. Woodbury, MN: Llewellyn Publications.

Weldon, Clodagh. 2006. *Fr. Victor White, O.P.: The Story of Jung's "White Raven."* Scranton, PA: University of Scranton Press.

Winnicott, D. W. 2006. *The Family and Individual Development*. New York: Routledge.

Wood, Michael. 2007. *In Search of Myths and Heroes: Exploring Four Epic Legends of the World*. Berkeley, CA: University of California Press.

Wurmser, Leon. 2007. *Torment Me, But Don't Abandon Me: Psychoanalysis of the Severe Neuroses in a New Key*. Lanham, MD: Jason Aronson.

Zelizer, Viviana A. 2007. *The Purchase of Intimacy*. Princeton, NJ: Princeton University Press.

JOURNAL OF
Sandplay Therapy

Subscribe Now

Name _____

Street _____

City, State, Zip/Postal Code, Country_____

Telephone _____ E-mail: _____

United States: $52.00 for one-year subscription (2 issues of same volume).

To subscribe to the *Journal of Sandplay Therapy* and for information regarding international subscriptions and past issues, please go to www.sandplay.org or email sta@sandplay.org

or write:
Journal of Sandplay Therapy
P.O. Box 4847
Walnut Creek, CA 94596
U.S.A.

Check or Money Order:
Payable in U.S. dollars to 'Journal of Sandplay Therapy' OR

Credit card:
Required for <u>international subscribers</u>. Please complete section below.

Card Type

VISA ❑   Mastercard ❑

Card Number_____ Exp. _____

Cardholder's Name _____

Signature _____

PO Box 4847, Walnut Creek, California 94596 USA
sta@sandplay.org • www.sandplay.org

FILM REVIEWS

Cinema: a New Possibility of Hope
THE 50TH SAN FRANCISCO INTERNATIONAL FILM FESTIVAL
26 April–10 May 2007

CATHLEEN ROUNTREE

Film is the greatest art form, at the moment, for penetrating deeply across the cultures, across the world. And it's the art form that has the lifeblood of the gestalt flowing through it right now. Film is making an incredible impact all over the world.

Thus spoke Peter Sellars, the gleefully eclectic multimedia visionary in his State of Cinema Address on April 29th at the San Francisco International Film Festival (SFIFF). Clad in a tangerine tunic and blue prayer beads worn as a necklace, Sellars' beatific Buddhist presence enveloped the rapt audience and, as did Tilda Swinton's address last year (Rountree 2006, 33–34), both tempered and highlighted festival proceedings.

In 2006, Sellars served as artistic director of Vienna's New Crowned Hope Festival, to which he invited international filmmakers, particularly from areas of conflict such as Cambodia, Paraguay, and Congo, to create — as he recounted for the SFIFF audience:

> the possibility to turn the page of history, and give people a new piece of paper on which to start writing again a new society. And at the same time have the spiritual, emotional and historical weight to acknowledge what has gone before.

Sellar's impassioned plea provides a resonant platform for honoring this cinematic milestone: SFIFF at 50 and its film offerings.

CATHLEEN ROUNTREE, Ph.D., is a film journalist and author of nine books, including the five-volume series on women's life stages: *On Women Turning 30, 40, 50, 60,* and *70.* She covers film festivals and writes for print and online publications, including *Documentary Magazine, Release Print,* and GreenCine. Her blog at www.WomeninWorldCinema.org closely follows global women's issues as addressed in films. *Correspondence:* 304 Bowsprit Drive, Aptos, CA 95003 USA, www.CathleenRountree.com, www.themovieloversclub.com, Cathleen@womeninworldcinema.org

In *Opera Jawa* (commissioned by Sellars), masterful Indonesian director Garin Nugroho updates an ancient Sanskrit love triangle utilizing poignant gamelan melodies and Javanese shadow puppetry. This "postmodern musical" serves as an affecting requiem for victims of violence and natural disaster.

A Few Days Later..., directed by and starring Iranian actress Niki Karimi, affords a minimalist portrait of artist and teacher Shahrzad, an educated, professional woman dealing with pressures in all aspects of her life. With its melancholic atmosphere, gorgeous landscapes, and a main character who drives through the countryside (sometimes aimlessly) as she pursues an existential questioning of life––the film approximates a feminist version of Kiarostami's *Taste of Cherry* (1997).

Documentarian Heddy Honigmann garnered the Festival's Golden Gate Persistence of Vision Award for a lifetime of cinematic achievement. In *Forever,* a melancholic celebration of the importance of art and beauty in our lives, Honigmann tenderly observes visitors to the famous Parisian cemetery Père-Lachaise — the final resting place of Gertrude Stein, Édith Piaf, Jim Morrison, Maria Callas, and many other luminaries. The film's vivid cast of characters intimately describes the comfort and inspiration they draw from visiting their deceased heroes (or, in a few cases, their non-famous spouses and relatives), proving that art, love, and beauty endure beyond death.

In *Flandres,* Bruno Dumont (*Humanité*) returns to the land of his childhood in northern France and raises his usual concerns about man's inhumanity to man. The often breathtaking mastery of his characters' nuanced emotions and expressions brings an immediacy to both his observational filmmaking and the viewers' experience of the film as a sense of eavesdropping. Dumont extends his battleground of human psychology to an actual combat zone — an unnamed desert locale and an unspecified enemy — and economically reveals war's atrocities on the frontlines and the concurrent emotional damage to loved ones at home.

Evocative of South Korean master director Im Kwon-taek's films (*Chihwaseon* and *Chunhyang*), Im Sang-soo's *The Old Garden* spans a turbulent seventeen-year period of South Korea's recent history in which the military police crushed the student-led protests, slaughtering several hundred students. A series of seamless flashbacks reveals the love story and heartbreak between an activist and an artist. Through a series of gorgeous tableaux, the film communicates a truth about memory: those few indelible moments, experiences both ecstatic and tragic, are what, in the end, give our lives meaning.

The Devil Came on Horseback, a devastating exposé of the genocide in Darfur, follows the young hero Brian Steidle, an ex-Marine who is learning to change the world through peaceful means, as he witnesses and photographs the worst imaginable atrocities. Nicholas Kristof, the *New York Times* columnist who has championed U.S. intervention in Darfur, reasons persuasively, "It's as if history gives us a chance to redeem ourselves after Rwanda, and yet we are failing again."

Part Tarkovsky, part early-Bergman, the stunningly beautiful *The Island,* directed by Pavel Lounguine, takes place on a minuscule island in the White Sea in 1976. Living the punitive life of a hermit in a Russian Orthodox monastery on his eternal quest for redemption, Father Anatoly divides his time between performing the Sisyphean task of shoveling coal into the monastery's insatiable fiery boiler and dealing with pilgrims who consider him a holy man and seer. The director wavers between revealing Anatoly as a lunatic and a saint. In an interview, Lounguine says, "This is a film about the fact that God exists. There comes a time in life when this becomes an important issue. Besides, I am trying to open up new genres in film, in this case the genre of the lives of saints" (Press Notes).

"Always expect the unexpected. Adapt that as a rule," advises 86-year-old Vig, the retired priest and university librarian, whose dream is to transform the castle he's inherited into a monastery. Imagine the contemplative quality of last year's *Into Great Silence* (Rountree 2006, 22), but with humor and deep emotion in place of cerebral remove, and you have *The Monastery.* Sensitively filmed by Pernille Rose Grønkjær, the dazzling cinematography discerns both a fairytale and dust-to-dust, ashes-to-ashes awareness.

The robust black-and-white cinematography of *The Violin* echoes the forceful content of Mexican first-time director Francisco Vargas's political allegory, in which Don Plutarco, the maimed patriarch of a group of peasant rebels, temporarily employs his violin-playing artistry to intrigue and distract the Captain of the Mexican army from his brutal treatment of the guerillas. *The Violin* illustrates Peter Sellars' affirmation in his State of Cinema Address that

> Cinema is part of a new possibility of hope. Cinema is part of gathering in small groups and reinforcing a sense of where we're coming from, but also where we're going. And what it means to hold the images in front of us to say, 'We're not there yet, but it's where we're going, so let's not stop here. Let's keep going there.' That idealism is actually what art was invented to do. To hold in front of you something that you aspire to.

ABSTRACT

CATHLEEN ROUNTREE, Ph.D. "Cinema: A New Possibility of Hope, THE 50TH SAN FRANCISCO INTERNATIONAL FILM FESTIVAL. 26 April–10 May 2007." JUNG JOURNAL: CULTURE & PSYCHE, 1:4, 97-100. Highlights of individual narrative and documentary films featured at the 50th San Francisco International Film Festival. In addition, Rountree references international theatre visionary Peter Sellars' State of Cinema Address presented at the Festival. Films and directors mentioned include *Opera Jawa*, Garin Nugroho; *A Few Days Later*, Niki Karimi; *Forever*, Heddy Honigmann; *Flandres*, Bruno Dumont; *The Old Garden*, Im Sang-soo; *The Devil Came on Horseback; The Island*, Pavel Lounguine; *The Monastery*, Pernille Rose Grønkjær; and *The Violin*, Francisco Vargas.

KEY WORDS

50th San Francisco International Film Festival, Peter Sellars, State of Cinema Address, Vienna's New Crowned Hope Festival, *Opera Jawa*, Garin Nugroho, *A Few Days Later*, Niki Karimi, *Forever*, Heddy Honigmann, SFIFF Golden Gate Persistence of Vision Award, Parisian cemetery Père-Lachaise, *Flandres*, Bruno Dumont, Im Kwon-taek and Im Sang-soo, *Chihwaseon, Chunhyang, The Old Garden, The Devil Came on Horseback*, Darfur, Brian Steidle, Nicholas Kristof, *The Island*, Pavel Lounguine, Russian Orthodox monastery, *Into Great Silence, The Monastery*, Pernille Rose Grønkjær, *The Violin*, Francisco Vargas, political allegory

BIBLIOGRAPHY

Rountree, Cathleen. 2006. "Commentary on The 49th San Francisco International Film Festival." *The San Francisco Jung Institute Library Journal*, 25:3, 20–35.

——. 2007. "Cinema Culture and Psyche: Film Festival Dispatches." JUNG JOURNAL: CULTURE & PSYCHE, 1:3.

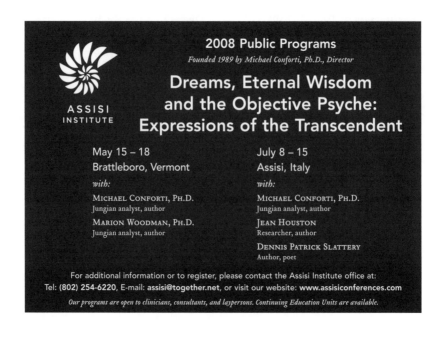

JUNG JOURNAL: CULTURE & PSYCHE, FALL 2007, VOL. 1, NO. 4, 101-107

INTERVIEW

The Shadow Within Friendship; An "Enterview" with Ann Lammers, Ph.D.

ROBERT S. HENDERSON

Henderson (RH): The title of your wonderful book is *In God's Shadow: The Collaboration of Victor White and C. G. Jung.* What do you mean when you say "God's Shadow?"

Ann Lammers (AL): This takes a preface, a detour into White's theology. Trying to talk with Jung about the nature of evil, its relationship to God and to the creation, was a major problem for White. Among other things, he could not agree with Jung that evil is as substantial as good. White held the orthodox Catholic view of evil, which says that the cosmos was originally and fundamentally good because it was created by God who is all good and all powerful. In this view, evil was not present at the origin of the world; it crept in when Adam sinned, as a kind of parasite. So evil threatens the creation, but only as a derivative power that distorts, corrupts, and diminishes the good.

This theory of evil is often referred to by Jung by its Latin shorthand, *privatio boni,* or the privation of good. Jung insisted that evil was present from the beginning along with good, and that it has as much reality and power as goodness does. He wants White to admit that the being of God (i.e., the God-image in the psyche) includes both good and evil. The all-good God may be a metaphysical truth, Jung says, but we know nothing

ANN LAMMERS is a psychotherapist practicing in Vermont. She received her Master of Divinity in 1982 from the General Theological Seminary, New York, and in 1987, she completed her Ph.D. in theology and psychology at Yale University. Her doctoral dissertation, *In God's Shadow: The Collaboration of Victor White and C. G. Jung,* was published in 1994 by Paulist Press. With help from Adrian Cunningham and Murray Stein, she edited *The Jung-White Letters* (Routledge, May 2007). She has recently begun to edit another volume for publication covering Jung's 32-year correspondence with James Kirsch, M.D. *Correspondence:* P.O. Box 8126, Brattleboro, VT 05304

Ann Lammers at Point Reyes

"objective" about metaphysical truths. They exist (if they do) outside the psyche's experience. Subjectively, Jung is sure that God (the God-image) includes an evil side — a shadow.

I had another reason to put the idea of God's shadow into my title. Victor White suffered, and his friendship with Jung foundered, partly because of church politics during his era. Catholics declare the church to be, in a mystical and sacramental sense, the body of Christ. When a faithful person such as Victor White is oppressed at the hands of his own hierarchy, he suffers from the church's shadow. To the extent that the church is symbolically identical with Christ, then the church's shadow is hard to tell from God's. Jung and White's friendship unfolded among the shifting internal politics of White's church and his Dominican Order. For me, therefore, their whole story takes place "in God's shadow."

While I was preparing the book for publication in the early 1990s, I was in friendly contact with C.G. Jung's son, Franz, who was an old man by then. I wrote to him excitedly when I came up with my title *In God's Shadow*. His immediate reaction surprised me: the words struck him as blasphemy! He scolded me vehemently: "We know nothing about God, how can you say God has a shadow?" I wrote back, defending the metaphor. I told him I meant it in the same nonliteral way as biblical texts referring to God's right hand, or mighty arm, or watchful eye. Once I reframed the phrase this way, Franz accepted the idea. He was very pleased when the book came out in August 1994.

RH: Why do you feel the Jung-White relationship is important for those interested in Jungian psychology?

AL: Recently, I came across a letter I'd written to Kate Hawes in October 2002 about the nature of the correspondence between Jung and White. We were discussing a permissions policy to apply to all the "third parties" mentioned in the letters. What I wrote to her partly answers the question, so I'll quote myself:

"These letters are not mainly about ideas (though they contain material for several dissertations). They are mainly about a relationship, and all the interwoven relationships that surround it. The two men have joined together in an adventure which is life-enhancing and life-threatening for them both. Their letters include the names of many other people, because these people shape their respective worlds, and they earnestly want to communicate to each other about their worlds.

"In the depths of Jung's psychology, where he and White met, professional and personal aspects of life aren't separable; they're entwined. Both aspects are given attention in these letters. The writers need to share all sorts of information about themselves in order to be understood. In the letters from the years when their relationship has soured, third party names drop out. Now Jung and White focus more narrowly on ideas; they cite authorities and argue over doctrines."

It's striking to me (continuing in the present, February 2007) that the pinnacle of the two men's *emotional* relationship is marked by the most intense *intellectual* activity on Jung's part. In mid-1948, Jung wrote a letter to White that is fairly incandescent with intuitive creativity. It marks the elaboration and deepening of Jung's theory of the Self, which led to his book *Aion*. On 21 May 1948, he enclosed in his letter a large diamond-shaped diagram, hand-drawn on the back of a manila envelope, which combined many aspects of the Self as a complex of opposites.

It seems to me that Jung's vulnerability toward his friend was at its deepest when he was allowing White to *feel with him in the realm of ideas*. White's virtual non-answer to this letter, and his apparent lack of appreciation for what Jung had sent him, might have been the first wound in their relationship. White was one-sidedly a thinking type, and Jung's thinking was (I believe) his third function at best. His intuition was saturated with feeling — this letter fairly aches with excitement about what he has been able to grasp intuitively. Preparing to present a major lecture at Eranos, he had to bring his thinking function into play and to organize his feeling-laden intuitions. The result was a many-faceted symbol, a diamond-shaped diagram of the Self, which (when I look at it) carries such a numinous charge, I am stunned when I consider how little White, in his thinking mode, was able to make of it.

Because of the intensity of their relationship, it's possible to treat the Jung-White letters to some degree (though I don't mean it physically) as a love story. It's certainly the story of a deep, abiding, emotionally important friendship on both sides. But these friends were temperamentally mismatched, and in mid-1948, their dissimilar temperaments threw them out of sync with each other, causing a shock on Jung's side that probably went too deep to be addressed with words. (They saw each other for a short visit once a year at most, so words, in the letters they exchanged, were all they had.) That unspoken injury, White's failure to feel with Jung, must have lingered and rankled. In the following year, when White reviewed Jung's 1948 lecture about the Self (to which the diamond-shaped diagram belonged), the magisterial dismissiveness of his review must have struck a sore nerve.

Their now-famous argument about whether or not evil is a "privation of good" begins in Jung's letter of 31 December 1949. There he calls White's review of his lecture on the Self "your *correctio fatuorum*" [punishment for fools]. Remarkably, though, the strength of the underlying relationship kept them in regular contact for seven years after this. Then comes their four-year estrangement, from 1955–1959, which came about from the accumulated emotional injuries on both sides, as much as from intellectual disagreements. Their handful of final letters to each other show that their deep connection still survived. They made a poignant effort to reconcile before White's death.

If people are interested in Jung's psychology, they should also be interested in the internal field — an intertwined field combining emotional and intellectual relationships — in which his creativity found room to grow. White's friendship held and nourished Jung's imagination as he created the complex interpretation of the Christ-symbol, central to his writing on the Self. When White failed to value what Jung had created, that injury did not halt Jung's creative process; it only drove it deeper. By putting obstacles in the way of Jung's feeling-intuitive drive, White forced him to defend his creation, strengthening it. But while all this was going on, their friendship endured, with a robustness that I find remarkable, as an emotional container. Jungians with an appreciation of object-relations may find something to reflect on here.

RH: Your work on the *Letters* brought you into contact with the Jung family. What was that like for you?

AL: It started long before I began editing *The Jung-White Letters.* In 1986, I was in my doctoral program at Yale's Religious Studies Department doing independent study in two fields, theology and psychology. It's hard to write a dissertation across disciplines, so I had decided to narrow my topic by studying the historical relationship between individuals whose dialogue bridged these fields. The two individuals I'd settled on were White and Jung.

I never actually set out to meet the Jung family. It happened because I so much needed to see White's letters to Jung. I'd heard that his letters were locked up and off-limits to researchers, but I had to try to see them. I wrote first to the head of the C.G. Jung Archive in Zürich, Dr. Glaus. The reply came not from him but from one of Jung's grandsons, Lorenz Jung. He declined my request: His grandfather, he wrote, "had wished his correspondence with White to remain confidential." Swallowing my disappointment, I wrote back, saying I understood, but might I ask a favor? If I could not see White's letters, maybe Lorenz Jung could. Would he kindly read them and answer some questions for me? I listed several questions — everything I could think of.

About a month passed. Then I received a long letter, not from Lorenz, but from C.G. Jung's son, Franz. Lorenz Jung had talked to his father about my request, and Franz Jung, a retired architect in his seventies, had taken it on himself to read through Victor White's long correspondence. His letter answered all my questions, point by point, and referred me to key pieces of Jung's and White's published work.

It was a tremendous gift. I was giddy, too, from the experience of writing to Beat Glaus and receiving a letter back from Lorenz Jung, and then writing to Lorenz and receiving a letter back from Franz. I played with the surreal notion that, if I wrote to Franz, the next letter I got would be from C.G. himself. No such magic occurred, but the seeds of a friendship were planted.

After further correspondence, Franz Jung permitted me to include his original letter in my dissertation. When the work was done, he asked me to send him a copy, which he immediately read and then handed on to Lorenz. On the strength of what they both saw in my work, in late 1989, the Jung heirs decided to release White's letters to the C.G. Jung Archive. By then, I was revising my dissertation for publication, and they wanted to give me access to White's letters to fill in a missing piece in my work.

What follows may seem like a diversion from the topic of meeting Jung's family, but it happens that the release of White's letters for scholarly research helped to deepen my friendship with Franz Jung. Events in 1989–1990 come into play here. (These events are described in *The Jung-White Letters*, "Editorial Note.") I didn't know all of this while it was happening, but I pieced it together afterward from conversations and letters.

Once, in 1992, when I was trying to understand why the Jung heirs had decided to release White's letters for research, Franz Jung read my attempts to write that history and exclaimed, with an emphasis bordering on exasperation, that White's letters were released for no other reason than my own doctoral work. (*"Es war Ihre Dissertation!"*) Of course I was, and am, overwhelmed to think this was partly true; however, it's clear that other factors also came into play.

In June 1990, Lorenz had received an unexpected letter from an English theologian, Adrian Cunningham, writing on behalf of White's legal heirs, the English Dominicans. Mr. Cunningham himself arrived a few weeks later, bearing a letter signed by the English Dominican Provincial, who gave him full authority over the papers of Victor White. He requested that copies of White's letters be turned over to him at once.

The Jung heirs hastened to comply; but with embarrassment, they found they could not hand over copies of White's letters. Early in the summer of 1990, Lorenz Jung, who had been handling the release of the letters to the ETH [*Eidgenössische Technische Hochschule Zürich*, or the Swiss Federal Institute of Technology, where Jung was a professor of psychology from 1933–1941], entered the hospital with a recurrence of cancer, and in the commotion, the letters were mislaid. (They would resurface in a locked cabinet at Lorenz's residence several months after his death.)

Facing these complicated circumstances, Franz Jung wrote to me at least twice during the summer of 1990. First, he informed me of Adrian Cunningham's letter, suggesting that I write immediately to the Provincial of the English Dominicans to ask if I could be allowed, also, to receive copies of White's letters. He added that his son was in the hospital. In August, he wrote again, with sorrow, that Lorenz had died. And he explained that, to everyone's confusion, White's letters could not be found. I wrote back with sympathy for the loss of his son. The mislaid letters concerned me very little; I assumed they would show up eventually. When the Jung-White letters were found early in 1991, the originals were given to the C.G. Jung Archive, and copies were distributed to Adrian Cunningham and to me.

So I flew to Switzerland in August 1991. Sitting at a Zürich train platform the day after arriving from California, I tried to prepare for a conversation with Franz Jung. This, our first meeting, might be my only chance to ask him about his father's relationship with White. I was thrilled, anxious, and jetlagged. In my canvas briefcase was my only copy of the Jung-White letters, together with a new, small tape recorder. I lifted the little briefcase onto an overhead rack and watched out the window for the station. There it was — *Küsnacht!*

But it was *Küsnacht/Goldbach,* not *Küsnacht/Zürich.* Not only was I at the wrong station, but also I'd left my briefcase on the train! There was nothing to do but walk to the other end of Küsnacht, which I did, getting to the long driveway of Seestrasse 228 half an hour later, sweating and thirsty. Then I stood at the huge doorway to ring the bell. Was it Franz Jung who came to the door? I believe it was his friend Els Glaser, and she came downstairs to meet me, invited me in, and cheerfully gave me a glass of water. Franz returned soon, after a second attempt to pick me up at the station. He bade me welcome and served me a slice of the apricot torte he had baked himself for the occasion. ("No sugar! Do you like it?")

When he heard I had lost the briefcase containing my copies of the long-sought letters between Jung and White, Franz looked sober, and he dropped his voice into a low register: "My father would have said, 'That is an omen!'" But we decided to overlook the omen. He then talked with me for almost two hours about his recollections of Victor White and his father. We made plans to meet again the next day to discuss the letters. To my amazement, the next morning at the lost and found of the main rail station I recovered my briefcase, missing only the tape recorder. A long conversation with Franz ensued that afternoon, and a long-distance friendship unfolded over the next five years, broken only by Franz's death. I remember him with deep affection.

JUNG JOURNAL
DONORS
July 1, 2006–June 30, 2007

The task of publishing a journal with high production values and articles in depth would not be possible without our loyal subscribers and generous additional support.

We gratefully acknowledge those who have given cash donations, silent auction donations, and/or donations to attend fundraising events.

Bonnie K. Abel
Marti J. Atkinson
Vicki Bailey
Michael Bala
David Barkley
Anita Barzman
Sandra W. Beddow
John Beebe
Katherine Betz
Susan Bostrom-Wong
Roberto R. Bours
Mary Boyvey
Katherine Bradway
Burk Braun
Carolyn Bray
Katherina Bruner
William Bundy
Ryan Bush
Leta Bushyhead
Robert Bushyhead
Susan Calfee
Kelly Cannon
Tessamarie Capitolo
Nerina Cecchin
Qi Re Kiki Ching
Rusa Chiu
Joan Chodorow
Bobby Christopher
Norma Churchill
Janet Wullner-Faiss Cloak
Betsy Cohen
O'Brien Colette
Sheryl Coryell
Susan Cross
Carl Culberson
Mary Culberson
Chris Cunningham
Lauren Cunningham

Patricia Damery
Elissa Davis
Zsolt Deak
Gayle Dearborn
Wayne K. Detloff
Diane Deutsch
Alexandra Dickerman
Donna Donohue
Mary Dougherty
Claire Douglas
Harold Dudley
Susan Dunn
Max Erdstein
Barbara Factor
Brian Feldman
Eric I. Field
Diana Fisher
Allen Flagg
Charlie Fleetham
Janet Flores
Millie Fortier
Ruth Foster
Lynn Alicia Franco
Karl Fredrickson
Don Freeman
Amy Kline Gage
Charlie Garfield
Marilyn Geist
Carol Gentry
Payam Ghassemlou
John L. Giannini
Lori Goldrich
Sandra Golvin
Baruch Gould
Gwendolyn Gowing
Ethne Gray
Robin Greenberg
Leslie Griffith

Adam Gruen
Gail Grynbaum
Mary Cay Gundry
Ciell Harrison
Deborah Harsh
Francis Hatfield
Justin Hecht
Christine Hejinian
Joseph L. Henderson
Steven Herrmann
Louise Heyneman
Anne N. Hoagland
Ann Hogle
George Hogle
Barbara Holifield
Kristina Holland
Valerie Hone
Walter S. Horn
Sandy Hurt
Shirley Scott Ireland
Amy Jessen
Don Hanlon Johnson
Steven Joseph
C. G. Jung Institute
    of San Francisco
Viera Kair
Eve Keihner
Steve B. Keihner
Claire Khouri
Barbara Kinsey
Jean Kirsch
Tom Kirsch
Paula Klimek
Liana Kornfield
Puddi Kullberg
Mike Kurokawa
Janet Laughlin
Margo Leahy

Sandra Lee
Dick Lemon
Michael S. Looney
Naomi Lowinsky
Jon Lucca
Sibyl F. Lundy
J. Linn Mackey
Rhonda Magee
Helen Marlo
Pat McCaffrey
Sandy McLerren
Carol McRae
Kathleen Meagher
Jack Meier
Amalia Mesa-Bains
Lilly A. Miningham
Phillip Moffitt
Anthony Muchnicki
K. Nadasi
Marilyn Nagy
Karen Naifeh
Gary Newsom
John V. Nicholas
Maria Jesus Noriega
Merry T. O'Donnell
Deborah O'Grady
Edward F. Pajak
Ruth Palmer
Jesse Patrick
Bonnie Payne
Richard Payne
Alexander Peer
Daniel Polikoff
Noelle Poncelet
John Powell

Nancy Powers
Neville Powers.
Alan Ptashek
J. F. Rea
Prather Rebecca
Barbara Kathleen Rector
Michael E. Reding
Jane Reynolds
William Rhodes
Stella Richards
Tom Richardson
Bill Riess
Janet Robinson
Fred B. Rogers
Jeanine A. Roose
Moore Rosemary
David Rosen
Rose-Emily Rothenberg.
Alan Ruskin
Susan Ruskin
Neil Russack
Suki Russack
Meredith Sabini
Katherine Sanford
Lynda Schmidt
April Sheldon
Peter L. Sheldon
Dyane Sherwood
Ellen Y. Siegelman
Dennis P. Slattery
Francis Slocumb
Margaret Smalzel
Cindy Spring
Marilyn Steele
Jane Alexander Stewart

Tina Stromsted
Barbara Stevens Sullivan
Mark Sullivan
JoAnn Szybalski
Helen Tait
Stephanie Taylor
Susan Thackrey
John Theede
Johanna Treichler
Dennis Turner
Maura Twohig
Dennis Turner
June Unfried
Barbara Van Slyke
Alan Vaughan
Inge Von der Hude
Jeanne Vonnegut
Michael Vonnegut
Louis Vuksinick
George Wagner
Suzanne Wagner
Mitch Walker
Kristin Walsh
Steve Walsh
Dick Ward
Karlyn Ward
Barbara W. Watkins
Wilfred H. Weeks, Jr.
Catherine White
Susan Williams
Scott Wirth
Steven Wong
James Yandell
Jane Zich
Alan R. Zopf

Lavender Party and Silent Auction Volunteers

Our June fundraiser at Patricia Damery's and Donald Harms' bio-dynamic lavender farm and vineyard overlooking the Napa Valley was a delightful gathering. Volunteers organized the event and prepared a delicious buffet and fragrant lavender lemonade. Their amazing organization and energy was an inspiration!

Thanks also to donations of wine and fabulous silent auction items, this event raised $6200.

Michael Bala
Ryan Bush
Norma Churchill
Patricia Damery
Jimalee Gordon
Robin Greenberg
Adam Gruen

Donald Harms
Lutrell Harms
Terry Harms
David Lerner
Jon Lucca
Jenna McRae
Marianne Morgan

Steven Nouriani
Neville Powers
Susannah Powers
Virginia Beane Rutter
Mark Sullivan

THE JOURNAL OF ANALYTICAL PSYCHOLOGY
VIIIth INTERNATIONAL CONFERENCE

Tradition and Creativity:
Reframing Analysis in a Changing World

Thursday 15th May to Sunday 18th May 2008
Hotel San Rocco, Orta San Giulio, Italy

'It is not possible to be original except on the basis of tradition' (D.W. Winnicott)

This residential conference offers an opportunity to consider the ways in which analytical psychology can make a creative response to the social, cultural and scientific developments of the early 21st century while maintaining its roots in the accumulated knowledge and experience of the analytic tradition.

Speakers will include Sue Austin, Stefano Carta, Massimo Giannoni, Christopher Hauke, Jean Knox, and Vittorio Linguardi. The opening address will be given, in Italian, by Umberto Galimberti. (It will be available in English prior to the address.)

The Conference will take place in the picturesque and romantic setting of Lake Orta, one of the smaller and most attractive lakes of Northern Italy. Situated approximately 40 mins from Milan Malpensa Airport, Lake Orta has inspired writers such as Balzac and Browning and, in 1882, was the setting for the inspirational meeting between Nietzsche and Lou Andreas-Salomé.

Address for a registration form and further information:
Journal of Analytical Psychology Conference
1 Daleham Gardens, London NW3 5BY
Tel 44+ (0) 20 7794 3640; Fax 44+ (0) 20 7431 1495. Email: journal.jap@btconnect.com

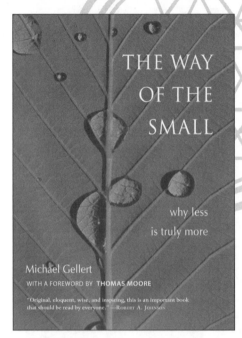